CHOOSE
JOY

CHOOSE JOY

Because Happiness Isn't Enough

KAY WARREN

Revell

a division of Baker Publishing Group
Grand Rapids, Michigan

© 2012 by Kay Warren

Published by Revell
a division of Baker Publishing Group
PO Box 6287, Grand Rapids, MI 49516-6287
www.revellbooks.com

Repackaged edition published 2020
ISBN 978-0-8007-3828-0
ISBN 978-0-8007-3826-6 (pbk.)

Printed in the United States of America

The Library of Congress has cataloged the original edition as follows:
Warren, Kay, 1954–
  Choose joy : because happiness isn't enough / Kay Warren.
      p.   cm.
  Includes bibliographical references.
  ISBN 978-0-8007-2172-5 (cloth)
  ISBN 978-0-8007-2177-0 (pbk.)
  1. Joy—Religious aspects—Christianity. I. Title.
BV4647.J68W37 2012
248.4—dc23   2011051196

Unless otherwise indicated, Scripture quotations are from the HOLY BIBLE, NEW INTERNATIONAL VERSION®. NIV®. Copyright© 1973, 1978, 1984 by International Bible Society. Used by permission of Zondervan. All rights reserved.

Scripture quotations labeled AMP are from the Amplified® Bible, copyright © 1954, 1958, 1962, 1964, 1965, 1987 by The Lockman Foundation. Used by permission.

Scripture quotations labeled CEV are from the Contemporary English Version © 1991, 1992, 1995 by American Bible Society. Used by permission.

Scripture quotations labeled GNT are from the Good News Translation—Second Edition. Copyright © 1992 by American Bible Society. Used by permission.

Scripture quotations labeled GW are from GOD'S WORD®. © 1995 God's Word to the Nations. Used by permission of Baker Publishing Group.

Scripture quotations labeled Message are from The Message by Eugene H. Peterson, copyright © 1993, 1994, 1995, 2000, 2001, 2002. Used by permission of NavPress Publishing Group. All rights reserved.

Scripture quotations labeled NASB are from the New American Standard Bible®, copyright © 1960, 1962, 1963, 1968, 1971, 1972, 1973, 1975, 1977, 1995 by The Lockman Foundation. Used by permission.

Scripture quotations labeled NCV are from the New Century Version®. Copyright © 1987, 1988, 1991 by Word Publishing, a division of Thomas Nelson, Inc. Used by permission. All rights reserved.

Scripture quotations labeled NJB are from THE NEW JERUSALEM BIBLE, copyright © 1985 by Darton, Longman & Todd, Ltd. and Doubleday, a division of Random House, Inc. Reprinted by permission.

Scripture quotations labeled NKJV are from the New King James Version. Copyright © 1982 by Thomas Nelson, Inc. Used by permission. All rights reserved.

Scripture quotations labeled NLT are from the Holy Bible, New Living Translation, copyright © 1996, 2004, 2007 by Tyndale House Foundation. Used by permission of Tyndale House Publishers, Inc., Carol Stream, Illinois 60188. All rights reserved.

Scripture quotations labeled Phillips are from The New Testament in Modern English, revised edition—J. B. Phillips, translator. © J. B. Phillips 1958, 1960, 1972. Used by permission of Macmillan Publishing Co., Inc.

Scripture quotations labeled TLB are from The Living Bible, copyright © 1971. Used by permission of Tyndale House Publishers, Inc., Wheaton, Illinois 60189. All rights reserved.

Special thanks to Elisa Fryling Stanford for help in manuscript preparation.

In keeping with biblical principles of creation stewardship, Baker Publishing Group advocates the responsible use of our natural resources. As a member of the Green Press Initiative, our company uses recycled paper when possible. The text paper of this book is composed in part of post-consumer waste.

green press
INITIATIVE

20 21 22 23 24 25 26   7 6 5 4 3

To
Kaylie, Cassidy, Caleb, Cole, and Claire
I cherish you

Contents

Contents

Those who plant in tears
    will harvest with shouts of joy.
                Psalm 126:5 NLT

Only the heart that hurts has
a right to joy.
                Lewis Smedes

Preface

When I wrote *Choose Joy*, I revealed that I had a close family member who was living with a mental illness. I spoke about the challenge of choosing joy in the face of a struggle that was very dark and scary at times—both for my loved one and for me. As you may know, our "struggle" became catastrophic loss when our twenty-seven-year-old son, Matthew, took his life in April of 2013 after two decades of intense, painful—even torturous—mental and emotional suffering. The news of his suicide seemed to fill the airwaves for a short period of time, and we were thrust into the public spotlight in ways we had always hoped to avoid.

The detailed circumstances of his death are private, but what I am comfortable telling you is that on the morning of April 5, 2013, I had very good reasons to believe Matthew had taken his life, although it wouldn't be confirmed until later that day. The night before I did not sleep, I was so full of anxiety and grief because I was pretty sure he had died. So when I got dressed that morning, I deliberately reached into my jewelry drawer and selected a necklace that said *Choose*

Joy. I was sick to my stomach, shaking from head to toe, and terrified that what I had dreaded had actually happened. But I put that necklace on because, somewhere in the dim recesses of my frozen mind, I was certain the only thing that would allow me to survive the loss of my son was what I knew and believed about God . . . and joy. That morning I possessed these three things: the settled assurance that God is in control of all the details of my life, the quiet confidence that *ultimately* everything is going to be okay, and the determined choice to give my praise to God—even on April 5, 2013.

These ensuing months of shattering grief and loss have severely tested those three convictions, and the opportunities to choose joy—or not—have been endless. I really believe that God allowed me to write *Choose Joy* before Matthew died to prepare me for what was ahead, so that when he died, I would have the tools I desperately needed to survive and even thrive during one of my life's most tragic losses.

Most of you will not face anything as devastating as the loss of a child due to suicide, but every single day you will face *something* that threatens your attempts to live with joy. Health problems, financial worries, marriage issues, loneliness, unresolved relational conflicts, anxiety about our nation or our world, stress over how your kids are turning out—the devil is at work nonstop to interfere with or interrupt your plans and dreams. Your primary task in life is to get to know God intimately and to send your spiritual roots deep into the soil of his love; to develop convictions and certainties about him that will become the source of your strength when happiness isn't enough.

I pray that *Choose Joy* will inspire you to know God better, to trust him more, and to become convinced that you too can choose joy!

PART 1

JOY Is My INHERITANCE

Embracing the Permission to Be Joyful

You made the team!
You've been awarded a scholarship!
We'd like to hire you!
Great job on closing that deal!
You've just won an all-expense paid vacation!
There's no sign of cancer!

These are some of life's sweetest moments—when all is right with the world, all your fondest hopes and wildest dreams come true, and your heart nearly explodes with happiness. You could make your own personal "it doesn't get any better than this" commercial.

But there are also other moments when nothing seems to go your way, everything that could go wrong does go wrong, and your fondest hopes and wildest dreams lie in shattered pieces at your feet. Those are the moments when your heart aches with the bitterness of unfulfilled longings, broken promises, or grief so powerful it threatens to take you to your knees.

Where does *joy* fit into these scenes from your life?

Sharing meaningful time with family and friends, having a great job, enjoying good health, being financially secure—aren't these the building blocks for a happy life? Most of us would say these happy moments create joy, don't they?

Probably everyone would agree that feelings of happiness are sometimes tough to come by so you better grab them when you can. Isn't that enough?

On the other hand, we're certain the painful moments rob us of joy; anyone who says they are experiencing joy as they stand at a graveside is only giving the socially correct answer, right? None of us believe them, but we nod our heads and say the right words so that no one knows that on the inside we doubt God's wisdom, his goodness, and his mercy.

Is joy really a possibility for messed-up and mixed-up pilgrims on this journey? Isn't *joy* just a biblical word that has nothing to do with real life?

Great questions. I mean, really great questions. I ought to know; they're my questions. I have a feeling you have asked similar questions—at least in your mind. You may never have felt comfortable voicing them out loud, but they have rolled around inside your head, especially in your most difficult moments.

Have you wondered why some people seem to experience deep and authentic joy in their daily lives—even in the toughest times—and others can't seem to find it no matter how hard they search? Many of us eventually give up the pursuit, assuming we were unfortunate enough to have been standing on the wrong side of the door when God was handing out joy. It has often seemed to me that only a few lucky people received the gift of joy and that fewer still know joy's "secret."

I'm here to say, I've learned that's just not true! Even though it may not feel that way to you at this moment, joy is available to you. You may be thinking, *I don't experience joy as much as other people do. It's just not my thing.* Or, *Joy means living in denial of all the pain in the world.* But as I've discovered in my own life, joy is not about your circumstances or about how you feel. It is definitely not about living in denial and ignoring sorrow or pain. Joy is something much deeper, richer, more stable, and more accessible than you might have thought.

That's the beauty of the joy God offers. You no longer need to live in fear or worry, because God's joy will always be available to you. In this world you will have trouble, Jesus says. But you can still take heart. You can still receive joy. You are not dependent on anyone or anything other than God and yourself to know joy.

There's one promise I want to give you as we start: I will be honest with you about my life and my search for joy—maybe more honest than you will find comfortable. I will not gloss over my doubts, failures, and sins, and I will admit to you—and myself—my sweaty, middle-of-the-night wrestling with God over issues of faith. I will let you into the internal workings of my faith in process because I find my own faith bolstered when I know someone else is struggling and sometimes succeeding in letting Christ be formed in them. Spiritual growth doesn't happen automatically and is rarely pretty; we will all be "under construction" until the day we die and we finally take hold of the "life that is truly life" (1 Tim. 6:19). So let's walk side by side for a while, and I'll share with you what I'm learning about how to choose joy every day . . . in the best and worst of times . . . in every moment.

—— ONE ——

Seeking a Life of Joy

He will yet fill your mouth with laughter
and your lips with shouts of joy.

Job 8:21

Pain is inevitable,
but misery is optional.
We cannot avoid pain, but we can avoid joy.

Tim Hansel

Because I grew up in a pastor's home, went to a Christian college, married a pastor, became a Bible teacher, and co-wrote a book on systematic theology for the average Christian, you might naturally assume that I have my spiritual act totally together and have this joy "thing" mastered. I wish I could say that was an accurate assumption, but truthfully, I wrote this book because I don't always have it all together! You and I share similar struggles and questions, and I need joy just as much as you do.

Joy does not come easily to me; I'm definitely more of a glass-half-empty kind of gal. In fact, I've struggled with low-level depression as far back as I can remember. As a little girl I was emotionally intense—I cried easily, agonized over the pain others felt, and carried the weight of the world on my small shoulders. So I'm not talking to you about joy from the perspective of one of those deliriously happy, peppy people who never have a down day. Some days I'm thrilled just to survive!

The Bible gives some commands that are extremely hard to understand and even harder to live out. One of the most difficult commands is to forgive our enemies. In light of the terrible cruelty and evil we can inflict on each other, this seems like asking an armchair athlete to climb Mt. Everest— impossible. The Bible also says not to worry about anything. *Anything? Really?* Many of us spend a good portion of every waking hour worried or anxious about something. How could God reasonably expect us not to worry? But to me, even harder than either of those two commands is the one found in James 1:2: "When troubles . . . come your way, consider it an opportunity for great joy" (NLT).

Are you kidding me? When trouble comes my way, my first thoughts aren't usually about experiencing great joy. My typical reaction is more along the lines of fear, panic, worry, and even hopelessness. At the very least, I reserve the right to gripe and moan about my troubles. Hardly an opportunity for great joy.

It's really because of my own struggles to live with joy that I began to explore why my experiences didn't match up with Scripture. I studied the life of Jesus Christ and observed the way biblical characters such as King David; Mary, the mother of Jesus; the apostle Paul; and James, the half-brother of Jesus, reacted to trouble and sorrow and hard times. For instance, the apostle Paul wrote in Romans 5:

> We continue to shout our praise even when we're hemmed in with troubles, because we know how troubles can develop passionate patience in us, and how that patience in turn forges the tempered steel of virtue, keeping us alert for whatever God will do next. In alert expectancy such as this, we're never left feeling shortchanged. Quite the contrary—we can't round up enough containers to hold everything God generously pours into our lives through the Holy Spirit! (vv. 3–5 Message)

I saw a Grand Canyon–sized gap between their lives and mine, and it began to bother me. It was clear that joy—even in pain—was something the biblical writers expected Christians to experience on a regular basis, but I wasn't. Wondering what was different about their faith that allowed them to respond to their circumstances with joy launched me on an intensely personal search. Why was there a discrepancy between my experiences and theirs? I needed to know how to bridge the gigantic gap that was keeping me from living a joyful life.

When troubles come your way, consider it an opportunity for great joy (NLT).

I'll fill you in on what I'm learning as we go along, but let me jump to the conclusion of the search and tell you the bottom line: *Joy is a choice.* Nothing I will say in the rest of this book is more critical to the way you live out your years than that small sentence. Joy is a choice. The level of joy you experience is completely and totally up to you. It is not dependent on anyone else—what they do or don't do, how they behave or don't behave. Joy cannot be manipulated by the actions of puny human beings. It is not dependent on the amount of sadness or suffering or difficulties you endure. Joy cannot be held hostage to fear, pain, anger, disappointment, sadness, or grief. At the end of any given day, the amount of joy you experienced is the exact amount of joy you chose to experience. You, my friend, are in charge. The sooner you embrace this pivotal reality, the sooner you can begin to live a more joyful life.

The Bell Curve of Joy

Each of us approaches the idea of joy differently. You may remember from a high school or college astronomy class the Gaussian Probability Distribution—yeah, probably not—but in simple English, think of a bell curve. At one end of the bell curve are people who don't struggle much to have joy. Their natural temperament is optimistic and upbeat—the glass is half full. Sometimes they really annoy me because they never stop smiling and they seem to float through life with a cheerful, carefree, lighthearted attitude. I mutter to myself, *I wonder if he'd be smiling so big if he had my problems.* Maybe he really is living a charmed life; life hasn't slapped him around a whole lot yet. But another possibility is that life *has* slapped him around and he has done some serious spiritual work and learned how to access joy every day. Regardless, some people are on the positive end of the bell curve.

The vast majority of us are in the middle of the bell curve. Life isn't awful; we're moderately happy, not too high and not too low. We don't normally get overly discouraged or depressed. We admit to feeling tired a lot, perhaps a bit bored by the routine, and sometimes even flat. Daily *joy*? I'm not so sure. But, we hastily add, nothing is really *wrong*.

As the bell curve moves downward, there is a smaller group of people at the other end. They are hiding—or not hiding—a cavernous well of depression. Getting out of bed every morning is a chore, and the pleasures of life are gone; smiling and laughing are hard to do. Joy has simply evaporated. That might be because of stress in a relationship, a job change, physical illness, or even deep grief or loss. While people with mild depression can bounce back fairly quickly, those traveling the hard road of profound loss often need years to process their grief before they find their emotional and spiritual equilibrium restored. But the accompanying depression can leave them feeling guilty because they know they're "supposed" to be joyful and they're not.

Depression might also be present because of a chemical imbalance. We don't talk about this much, but many Christians battle depression and stress because of a biochemical imbalance. Some people have bipolar disorder, characterized by dramatic mood swings between periods of wild euphoria and disabling depression. Schizophrenia, personality disorders, and many other forms of mental illness—some mild, some severe—plague Christian families just as often as non-Christian families. Physical disability is obvious to the casual observer, but mental brokenness can hide beneath a "normal"-looking exterior. My friend Shannon Royce calls this having a "hidden disability."[1] Unfortunately, because of our innate desire to deny our problems and the hardline stance of those who believe any psychological disruption is mostly a matter of poor discipleship, Christians are often reluctant to talk about mental health issues. This leaves millions suffering alone, ashamed, and, worst of all, unsupported by the church. The stigma is real, and it hurts.

As this curve continues, there's an even smaller group of people at the far end who are contemplating suicide. For some of you, you've given life your best shot, and it's just not enough anymore. You're worn out from the struggle to survive another day, and escaping your painful circumstances has begun to dominate your thoughts. You may even wonder if your family would be better off without you. You've certainly thought that *you* would be better off without experiencing such pain. Joy is as alien to you as a foreign country. It's so far off in the distance that you believe you will never reach it again, nor are you sure you have the energy to try. You find your struggle extremely difficult to talk about, especially if you're a Christ follower; if mentioning mental illness at church is a risky topic, then talking about suicide or suicidal thoughts can be the ultimate taboo in church.

It's possible you're reading this book because someone who cares very much for you is aware of the enormous battle you're fighting and longs for you to experience joy once more. As John Eldredge says, "The story of your life is the story of a long and brutal assault on your heart by the one who knows what you could be and fears it."[2] The enemy of your heart, Satan, does not want you to leave the place of despair, but the lover of your wounded heart, Jesus Christ, has a better plan for you, and it includes joy.

You were meant for something more. You were meant to experience a life of joy.

Wherever you are on the bell curve, God has a tender word of encouragement for you: There is concrete, genuine hope for joy in your life. Even if you are in the middle of despair right now, you can experience joy. It is not out of your reach! Happiness in and of itself will never be enough; it's simply too flimsy, too unreliable, too unpredictable. You were meant for something more. You were meant to experience a life of joy.

Created for Joy

I love a book Lewis Smedes wrote many years ago called *How Can It Be All Right When Everything Is All Wrong?* Smedes writes, "You and I were created for joy, and if we miss it, we miss the reason for our existence! Moreover, the reason Jesus Christ lived and died on earth was to restore us to the joy we have lost. . . . His Spirit comes to us with the power to believe that joy is our birthright because the Lord has made this day for us."[3] Jesus died to *restore the joy* that is our inheritance, the joy we lost when Adam and Eve rebelled against God and set the stage for our personal spiritual rebellion.

The good news is that when we realize we've been living in spiritual rebellion against God—not necessarily through gross, terrible actions but by an attitude of "I don't need you, God"—we have the opportunity to receive Jesus Christ as our Savior and Lord. And along with Jesus Christ, we receive his Holy Spirit (Gal. 4:4–7). And with the Holy Spirit comes this beautiful gift of joy, our birthright—not one option out of many but our *birthright* (see Gal. 5:22).

God *created* us to be joyful. There's really no doubt about it. But God has left the decision whether to access that joy up to us. You and I get to decide if we're going to choose joy—created by God, bought and paid for by Jesus's death, given as a personal gift from the Holy Spirit—or not.

When you think about it like that, it's hard to imagine why any of us would ever refuse God's gift of joy. But sometimes we do.

Parallel Train Tracks

I used to think that life came in waves: There was a wave of good and pleasant circumstances followed by a wave of bad and unpleasant circumstances, with a lot of ebb and flow in between. Or life was a series of hills and valleys; sometimes we're up, then we're down. But I've come to realize that life is much more like a set of parallel train tracks, with joy and sorrow running inseparably throughout our days.

Every day of your life good things happen. Beauty, accomplishment, pleasure, fulfillment, and perhaps even excitement occur. That's the track of joy. But every day of your life also holds disappointment, challenges, struggles, and perhaps even losses for you or those you love. That's the track of sorrow. Most of us try to "outsmart" the sorrow track by concentrating our efforts on the joy track, as if by our positive outlook or outright denial of reality we can make the sorrow track go away. That's impossible, because joy and sorrow will always be linked. And in the strange paradox of the universe, at the exact moment you and I are experiencing pain, we are also aware of the sweetness of loving and the beauty still to be found. Likewise, at the exact moment we are full of delirious delight, we have the nagging realization that things still aren't quite perfect. No matter how "positive" we think or how hard we try to visualize only happiness, the sorrow track remains.

One of our toughest challenges in life is to learn how to live on both of those tracks at the same time.

But there's hope! Look ahead with me.

My young grandsons are train fanatics, so I often take them to a quaint outdoor train station where Amtrak stops many times a day. When the ticket agent isn't looking and the coast is completely clear, we stand on the train tracks together and look ahead as far as we can see, hoping to catch the very first sign of an approaching train. As we stand on the tracks and stare into the distant, bright horizon, those parallel tracks become one, no longer distinguishable as two separate tracks.

That's the way it will be for us too. During our lifetime, we "stand on the tracks" looking for signs of Jesus Christ's return. We watch for the sights and sounds that will alert us that his appearance is very close. We stare into the horizon, hoping to catch a glimpse of him. One day, in the brightness of his coming, we will meet him face to face. And when we do, the tracks of joy and sorrow will merge. The sorrow will disappear forever, and only the joy will remain. And everything will finally make complete sense. But until that day comes, we live with the parallel tracks of joy . . . and sorrow.

The Definition of Joy

Why are we so reluctant to believe that joy can be a reality for us? I can think of several possible reasons.

The first is that most of us don't have joy models. We don't know many people who have bridged the gap between their experience and what Scripture teaches. Most people we look at are swimming, just like us, in deep waters of very little joy.

Do you think you can name two people who live a life of joy the way the Bible talks about it? Some of you will instantly raise your hands and say, "Absolutely! I know tons of people who are joyful!" I don't mean people who are merely natural extroverts and smile and laugh a lot. I mean men and women who embody the James 1 kind of response to troubles: those who consider it an opportunity for great joy. That might change the number of joyful people you think you know. So let's keep going. Can you think of five people? How about ten people? (I feel sort of like Abraham bargaining with God to save Sodom and Gomorrah!) I seriously doubt that many of you can honestly name ten people who live a joyful life. A few years ago I tried to come up with a list of people who embody what it means to live with joy. I finally thought of two people; one of them was dead, and the other one wasn't me! Without role models to follow, we face a daunting task to figure out what it means to live with joy.

Another reason we're hesitant to believe that joy is within our reach is because we examine our own lives and see how far off we are from the "consider it great joy" response. We say to ourselves, *One of these days I'll go after joy, but not today. I mean, if it falls into my lap, that's great. But I'd be happy just to get through today. Really, I'd be thrilled just to get a good night's sleep! Joy is too big a stretch for me right now.*

So based on the facts that we don't see joy modeled for us and that our own life experience doesn't match what we read in the Bible, many of us have concluded that joy is not going to happen for us. If it does, it will be a total surprise. It will not be anything we can control.

That's why our definition of joy is crucial. If our definition is inadequate, we can wrongly assume that joy and happiness are synonymous and that having happy feelings must mean we are joyful—or that the lack of happy feelings must mean we don't have joy. We spend the day at an amusement park, or a sporting event, or have a fantastic vacation and conclude that the happy feelings we're experiencing equal joy; or we observe someone who always seems upbeat and optimistic and think they have joy.

Not necessarily. You can't see into their heart. You can't see into their life to know how they respond when tough times come. You're looking at the face they present to the world, and you're concluding that's what joy is.

But if joy is not warm, fuzzy feelings or a smiling face, and it is not dependent on circumstances, what is it?

A few years ago I read a quote by Paul Sailhamer, who said that joy comes from knowing God is in control of our lives.[4] I liked that a lot, but I wanted more words around it to adequately express what I believe Scripture teaches about how to live a joyful life. I've written a definition of joy and memorized it so I can remind myself of the powerful truths when I'm feeling shaky: Joy is the settled assurance that God is in control of all the details of my life, the quiet confidence that ultimately everything is going to be all right, and the determined choice to praise God in all things.

Did you catch that? Joy is a settled conviction ABOUT God. It's a quiet confidence IN God. And joy is a determined choice to give my praise TO God.

> *Joy is the settled assurance that God is in control of all the details of my life, the quiet confidence that ultimately everything is going to be all right, and the determined choice to praise God in all things.*

I'm going to repeat this definition throughout the book because it needs to seep into your soul. My prayer is that you will memorize it too and that it will come to your mind when your world seems to be falling apart. I know how profoundly my life is changing as I develop a settled conviction *about* God and his goodness. My confidence *in* God is growing as I trust that he is working behind the scenes to fit all the details of my life into his good plan. And my determination to give my praise *to* God is slowly leading me to the joy I've always longed for. I want the same for you!

When I say, "Everything will be all right," it's not the equivalent of saying, "Don't worry, be happy" or some other nifty little phrase. Believing that ultimately everything is going to be all right takes into account car accidents, cancer, bankruptcy, miscarriage, depression, and every other grief we face. Choosing to believe that God is always working, knitting together the fragments of our lives, always in control of it all, means that life *will* work together for our good and his glory.

Of course, we want all the answers now, today, this moment. And we want more than simple answers. We want explanations in triplicate with a certification that God is qualified to make those decisions, thank you very much. That's why the word *ultimately* is in our definition of joy. God doesn't promise answers or explanations on demand. He promises joy.

So joy is much more than external things. It's much more than that happy, giddy feeling that may come every once in a while. The joy that God speaks of in his Word is something you can count on. It has nothing to do with the circumstances of our lives—and that, I've discovered, is very good news.

In the chapters to come, we will look at how we know God created us for joy and how Jesus's life of joy and sorrow gives us permission to choose joy even in the midst of pain. We'll also look at how to develop habits of the mind and heart that free us to choose joy every day in our thoughts, words, and interactions with others.

Joy is not just a nice add-on to the Christian life, the bow on top of the package. It is God's *purpose* for your life. It's time to embrace it!

—— **PRAYER** ——

Father, I want to choose joy in my life. Rekindle hope in my heart. Help me to keep seeking the joy that belongs to me in Jesus Christ. In the name of Jesus, amen.

—— **FOR REFLECTION AND APPLICATION** ——

1. What do you allow to hold you back from living a life of joy?

2. Take a minute to read the definition of joy on page 27. Be still and quiet as you reflect on the words. Which words are easiest to accept into your life? Which are the hardest words to access?

TWO

Showing Our True Colors

Our mouths were filled with laughter,
  our tongues with songs of joy.
Then it was said among the nations,
  "The LORD has done great things for them."

Psalm 126:2

I would believe in their salvation if they looked a little more like people who have been saved.

Friedrich Nietzsche, commenting
on the Christians he knew

James, the half-brother of Jesus, who wrote the Epistle of James, did not accept that Jesus was the Messiah during Jesus's lifetime, but later he became a pastor and a pillar of the early church. Tradition tells us that he was martyred for his faith, so I'm eager to listen to what this man, who

31

penned the famous words that are the basis for this book, has to say. He is certainly someone who put his money where his mouth was. He wrote in James 1:2–4:

> Consider it a sheer gift, friends, when tests and challenges come at you from all sides. You know that under pressure, your faith-life is forced into the open and shows its true colors. So don't try to get out of anything prematurely. Let it do its work so you become mature and well-developed, not deficient in any way. (Message)

James says that in tough times our "faith-life is forced into the open and shows its true colors." That's a rather daunting thought: No matter what you *say* you believe, or what others *think* you believe, there's no hiding or pretending when the bottom falls out—when you receive a dreaded diagnosis, a loved one dies, your finances collapse, your kids decide to make a mess out of their lives, someone goes to prison, or mental illness destroys a relationship.

The faith-life I claim to have is revealed in those moments—not to God, because he already knows the true state of my heart, but to me. My true colors can no longer be hidden beneath the Sunday smiles or the polite exchanges with a neighbor at the mailbox. Suddenly, what lurks below the waterline of my soul is uncovered, and all my great statements of faith are worthless. What matters in those times is what I *do*.

Sometimes our reaction to a difficult situation is so far from a biblical response that we step back in shock and say, I thought I was a better Christian than that. I thought I was a more mature believer. I thought I had more oomph in my faith. I've got nothing! There's not much there at all. As painful as it is to become aware of the holes in our faith, we can be grateful that tough times give us an accurate report of where we need to change and grow.

But there is another unexpected benefit that comes when my faith-life is brought out into the open through painful circumstances: A watching world gets to see what believing in God really means. In Philippians 2:14–15, the apostle Paul says, "Do everything readily and cheerfully—no bickering, no second-guessing allowed! Go out into the world uncorrupted, a breath of fresh air in this squalid and polluted society. Provide people with a glimpse of good living and of the living God. Carry the light-giving Message into the night" (Message). Another translation says, "among whom you shine like stars in the dark world" (NCV).

When the sky falls in and we are thrown into chaos, our faith-life is suddenly on display for everyone—neighbors, friends, unbelieving family, and co-workers—to see. And the Bible says our faith-life should provide a stark contrast to the life of unbelievers, so much so that it would be like looking at a brilliant star against the inky blackness of a dark night sky—you can't help but notice the difference.

Many friends and acquaintances look at you with avid curiosity: How does a Christian respond in this situation? What does a person who goes to church every week and has one of those fish stickers on the back of their car do when bad stuff happens to them? Often they are really asking the questions not to judge you or to criticize you but because they genuinely want to know if being a Christian makes a practical difference in your life. When you react exactly the same way they would in a crisis, they can't help but wonder, Why in the world would I need their God? We have to ask ourselves the same hard question: If being a Christian makes no difference in the way we respond to problems, what good

33

is our faith? What have we gained by going to church every weekend, attending Bible studies, memorizing Scripture, and sending our kids to Christian school if, when trouble comes, we're just like everyone else?

This takes us back to our image of the parallel train tracks of sorrow and joy. When trials expose our faith-life, will others see us embracing both the joy and the pain of our life? We do not need to live out one and deny the other. Those around us need to recognize that both of these elements are part of life, and both give us hope for heaven.

Building a Stronger Faith

As I've already told you, I struggle to choose joy as my initial response to bad news. My first reaction is usually worry or anxiety, not joy, not thanking God for this "gift." And when I see that kind of reaction in myself, I am disappointed to realize how far I still have to go to be a mature woman of God.

But that's exactly the point James is making. The only way to grow up spiritually—to become mature and well-developed in our faith—is to go through the fire of testing, trials, and troubles. An untested faith is an unreliable faith. We hate the process of refining that makes us like Jesus Christ in our character because it involves pain and sorrow and stress and upheaval. Ronald Dunn says, "Why is the struggle so relentless? Because God wants to change us, and we don't want to be changed."[1] All of us want the *product* of trials and pain—maturity—without having to go through the *process*. But James warns us not to try to wriggle out of the hard times too soon; if we do, we will short-circuit the process and remain immature. I don't want to be a spiritual or emotional infant. Do you?

Time for another true confession. I'll admit I've told God, *I'm okay with staying a spiritual baby; I can live with remaining immature and underdeveloped because growing hurts!* But in my heart of hearts, that's not what I want. I want my faith-life to be sturdy and strong, mature and well-developed. I'm willing to let trials and troubles expose my faith-life so that I'll know to stay on the path until I'm finished, not just for my own benefit but for those who are watching my life.

If being a Christian makes no difference in the way we respond to problems, what good is our faith?

A watching world of friends, family, neighbors, co-workers, and casual acquaintances has questions about spiritual matters, especially as they relate to suffering and the presence of evil in the world and in their own lives. They are misinformed and confused about God, Jesus, the Holy Spirit, and the Bible. How we respond to trials—hopefully, like a star shining brightly in a dark sky—can earn us the opportunity to speak to their questions and accurately reflect to them who God really is.

Acts 16:16–34 gives an account of Paul and Silas imprisoned unjustly in Philippi for healing a demon-possessed young girl. After they were arrested, they were severely beaten and thrown into an inner cell where their feet were locked in stocks. The Bible says that around midnight Paul and Silas were praying and singing hymns to God and "the other prisoners were listening to them" (v. 25) when a severe earthquake shook the foundations of the prison, causing the prisoners to be freed from their chains.

It was customary for a jailer to commit suicide if his prisoners escaped, knowing the authorities would kill him anyway for his failure to secure those left in his care. That night, when the jailer was preparing to stab himself with his sword in response to the open prison doors, Paul shouted that they were all still in their cells. The Bible records the jailer's astonishment; he trembled and fell before Paul and Silas asking, "Sirs, what must I do to be saved?"

Then Paul and Silas—having earned the right to testify to who God is by their response to an unjust beating and imprisonment—told this jailer how he and his family could be saved. The jailer and his household followed Jesus Christ and were baptized. The account ends with this verse: "The jailer brought them into his house and set a meal before them; he was filled with joy because he had come to believe in God—he and his whole family" (v. 34).

I'm not convinced that I would have responded the way Paul and Silas did. I wish I could confidently say that I would have been praying and singing hymns at the top of my lungs, but I think I might have been weeping and wailing at the top of my lungs—letting everyone know that an injustice had been done and that somebody had better make it right quickly!

But not Paul and Silas. Their faith-lives were exposed for a watching world of felons and jailers to observe, and their true colors were revealed. They shone brilliantly like stars in the black-velvet night sky of their prison chains, and in so doing, they made God look really good—so good that a hardened jailer, used to the phony-baloney protests of innocence from criminals, knew something was VERY different about these men . . . and their God. He wanted what they had, and he wanted it for his family as well. Their settled assurance about God, their quiet confidence that ultimately everything would be all right, and their determined choice to praise God in all things opened the door of salvation for the jailer and his loved ones.

What did the jailer gain from his encounter with Paul and Silas? Not only salvation but joy!

The Watching World

What do you think the answer would be if you asked your friends, "Does God smile? Does he smile at you?" Many people—even Christians, if we would admit it—believe that God is a grumpy old man having a bad eternity (day) sitting up in heaven watching with his eagle eyes for ways to squish the tiniest bits of happiness we might find. *Smile? Probably not. Smile at me? Not if he knows what I'm really like.*

The world has a skewed view of Jesus as well. Was there ever a more maligned, misunderstood, and misrepresented figure in history than Jesus Christ? He is alternatively revered as the Savior of the world, the restorer of broken hearts, minds, and relationships, and reviled as the single most disruptive person ever to live, blamed for global wars, nationalistic opportunism, as well as interpersonal conflict.

When it comes to the Holy Spirit, there's total confusion among non-Christians. Who or what is a "Holy Spirit"? Visions of Casper the Friendly Ghost, or the Haunted Mansion at Disneyland, or the tongue-tied Mr. Bean ("the Holy Spicket") come to mind—it just sounds weird and spooky or goofy.

Most people also believe the Bible is a book of doom and gloom, full of tedious, outdated rules that don't make sense in our ultrasophisticated world of technology and innovation. Or they're afraid to read the Bible, fearing they won't be able to make sense of what they read or assuming they will be bombarded with words of condemnation, shame, and guilt.

A watching world needs to hear from us that God personifies joy. They need to know that Jesus was a man of joy as well as a man of sorrows. They need to know that the Holy Spirit gives us joy as a birthright to claim. They need to know that the Bible is a book of joy, with more references to joy, laughter, and merriment than to tears, sorrow, and sadness. Remember, we have to constantly ask ourselves, *Why would they believe God created joy, or Jesus was a man of joy, or the Holy Spirit gives joy, or the Bible is a book of joy if all they have to evaluate is my life? Am I perpetuating the myth that God is a God of sorrow because I can't access the life of joy he intended for me?*

In this season of my life, I'm even more aware that my faith-life is on display. For a long time I wanted to live a joyful, passionate life so that my children would have a strong role model as they developed their own faith-lives. But now I have grandchildren . . . I have nieces and nephews . . . I have young friends who look up to me . . . and it's more important than ever to show them the way to a life of joy—not happiness, but joy. I want my kids to be able to say, "My mom had a lot to deal with, but she overcame her personality. She didn't let her struggles define her. And at the end of the day, my mom was a woman of joy." I want my grandkids to be able to say, "My grammy loved me, and she made me feel special every time I was with her." I want my nieces and nephews to be able to say, "Aunt Kay was a little quirky, but she loved Jesus, and she was a woman of joy." I want the young women I work with to be able to say, "Kay wasn't perfect, but she found her joy in the Lord, even when she had many reasons to be sad." When the people who are watching me most closely make their short list of people who live with joy, I want to be on that list. Don't you want to be on somebody's short list?

Dancing with Shouts of Joy

By the way, in case you're wondering about the answer to the question I posed a few paragraphs back—*Does God smile at you?*—here's his answer:

> Yahweh your God is there with you, the warrior-Saviour. He will rejoice over you with happy song, he will renew you by his love, he will dance with shouts of joy for you. (Zeph. 3:17 NJB)

He doesn't just smile at you . . . he sings and dances with shouts of joy for you! My friend, he knows all about you. He knows how often you fail to get it right; he knows the times you earnestly desire to shine like a star on a dark night but don't quite make it. He knows the truest intentions of your heart; he sees where you're trying. He's keenly aware of the brutal pain that has ripped you into pieces; his heart aches with yours as you struggle to accept the process that makes you mature. He knows what no one else will ever know. And his response to all he sees within you . . . within me? This makes me weep. *He dances for us with shouts of joy.*

This is the God I want a watching world to know through me.

—— **PRAYER** ——

Father, I am struggling right now with the realization that troubles expose my faith-life; I'm not sure I really want my family, my friends, or my co-workers to know that about me. Help me to focus not on the ways I fail to accurately represent you to them but on your delight in me. Help me to draw closer to you so that I can build a stronger faith-life that includes joy in all things. In Jesus's name, amen.

—— **FOR REFLECTION AND APPLICATION** ——

1. What does your faith-life reveal about the depth of your relationship with God?

2. How does it make you feel to understand that God dances over you with joy? Is that easy for you to believe? Why or why not?

── THREE ──

Rediscovering Jesus,
the Man of Joy

I have told you this so that my joy may be in you and that
your joy may be complete.

John 15:11

It is the heart that is unsure of its God that is afraid to laugh.

George MacDonald

I think one of the reasons we forget that the Bible is a
book of joy is that we don't see Jesus, the main character
in the Bible, as a man of joy. Many of you know Jesus
well already. He's been there on your best days, days when
your heart was ready to explode with excitement. This is
the top. This is the pinnacle. I am so happy! And Jesus was
with you.

But Jesus has also been with you in the worst of times, times when you thought your heart was going to disintegrate from sorrow, when the pain was so overwhelming that you didn't know how you were going to survive the next minute, let alone the rest of your life. He has been there.

The reason Jesus can comfort us in sorrow is because he, too, suffered. Isaiah 53:3 says, "He was despised and rejected by men, a man of sorrows and familiar with suffering." It's easy to conclude from this passage that Jesus was *just* a man of sorrows. But if we look at him only through that lens, we're going to sell him short, because Jesus was also a man of joy.

And Jesus Laughed

God created the heavens and the earth, as well as humankind; unfortunately, our first human father and mother rebelled against God, leading to sin and sorrow being unleashed on our planet. As part of a plan far beyond our finite understanding, God the Father gave Jesus the role of becoming the Savior of the world to restore the terminally ruptured relationship between us and God. In that role, Jesus would leave the perfection of heaven and come to earth, where he would know immense suffering and pain and sorrow and heartache and betrayal and loss. He would become a man of sorrows. But in his essence, Jesus was a man of joy.

This is a critical point: In Jesus's *role*, he was a man of sorrows. But in his *essence*—his unchanging nature—he was a man of joy. In fact, the Bible tells us, "The Son of man came, enjoying life" (Luke 7:34 Phillips). I love that! The Son of Man didn't come bent over in pain. He didn't arrive with a scowl on his face, a killjoy who couldn't survive without his box of tissues. He came eating and drinking and loving life—"feasting," as another version says.[1]

So why is it that throughout history Jesus has been portrayed as sad, serious, somber? Why have we flattened Jesus into a one-dimensional character instead of understanding that he was both a man of sorrows and a man of joy?

Consider the most common images of Jesus, such as the sanitized image of Jesus's head that hangs in Sunday school classrooms all over America. This was the picture I grew up with in my church, and you may have too. In this image, Jesus's hair is perfectly styled, with soft curls framing his face. There's no sweat or grit or imperfection on his face, not a single enlarged pore on his cheeks. No pimples, no wrinkles, no laugh lines around his mouth; there's not even a hint of a smile on his smooth face. As a kid, I remember thinking I had to be very serious around the Jesus painting; you could laugh anywhere else in the room, but not next to Jesus!

In Jesus's role, he was a man of sorrows. But in his essence—his unchanging nature—he was a man of joy.

While many evangelical churches display the "gentle Jesus, meek and mild, who wouldn't harm a flea" painting, other churches fill their sacred spaces with images of Jesus in his most agonizing moments. In fact, almost all fine art throughout the centuries portrays him on his most grievous day on earth—the day he was beaten and bloodied, with a crown of thorns viciously thrust into his scalp; the day he collapsed under the weight of the wooden cross he carried on his lacerated back through the streets of Jerusalem; the day he was brutally murdered.

43

Some of the well-known portrayals of Jesus focus on the aftermath of his crucifixion, when he was taken down from the cross, limp and broken. One of the most emotionally stirring pieces of art is Michelangelo's *Pietà*, with the lifeless body of Jesus draped across his mother's lap. Every parent resonates with the pathos of his mother's desire to gather the dead child of her womb close to her heart one more time.

I know why fine art has captured Jesus in his most painful moments—there's no mystery here. It's why he came to earth; Jesus came to die. He came to be our Savior, and being our Savior meant pain. Hurt. Sorrow. Suffering. To record that in art is perfectly appropriate; it really happened, and it was even worse than it appears.

The problem is that we don't balance those graphic images of Jesus with other lighthearted images, and we are left to conclude that his was a life of sorrow that ended in tragedy. In my efforts to learn how to choose joy—even in this imperfect world—I set out to discover images of Jesus that show him in the lighter moments that reflect his essence, not just his role.

The first one I found is probably the most famous. It's called *The Laughing Christ*. You won't believe where it was first seen: the January 1970 issue of *Playboy*. (I do not expect you to go find that issue to verify that I'm telling you the truth. Just believe me.) Hugh Hefner was captivated by the idea that Jesus could laugh. It was so startling to him, so against what he had seen all his life, that he published it.

Another joyful picture is called *The Laughing Jesus*. I tried to find it at a Christian bookstore a few years ago, and they told me they didn't carry it. It was a special order, and I'd have to wait three weeks. I thought, *What's going on here? I can get more art than I can shake a stick at of Jesus suffering, wounded, bleeding, dying. But I can't find a single picture to put in my house that shows him laughing and enjoying life?*

Jesus was a vibrant, compassionate man, a man of both sorrow and joy who could enter fully into life with all its brokenness. That sounds like someone I'd like to get to know. If he was a man of sorrows *and* could experience joy, maybe I can too.

So I want to shake up the perceptions of Jesus that you've been taught your entire life. I'll let Jesus prove it to you himself through his attitude, his words, and his actions. We've been talking about the lack of joy role models—there is none better than Jesus Christ. His life is a model for any of us who are seeking a life of joy.

A Man of Joy through His Attitude

Three of the Gospels record an incident when parents crowded near to Jesus, holding out their infants and children for him to touch them (Matt. 19; Mark 10; Luke 18). Scripture says that he "took the children in his arms, put his hands on them and blessed them" (Mark 10:16). While parents today are especially cautious about strangers being around their children, parents have always been wary of exposing their children to danger. The parents who were so eager to have Jesus touch and hold and bless their children must have sensed that he had a tender heart toward their little ones.

Even if the parents were confident in Jesus's ability to charm the kids, that doesn't mean that the children would automatically be comfortable around him, but there's no record of them shrinking away from his touch. We all know that kids have a way of sensing who the fun people are and

45

the people they don't really want to be around. My grand-kids are the joy of my heart, and we love being together, but I suspect my grandkids love their papa in a special way. The other day four-year-old Caleb whispered in Rick's ear, "Papa, you're my favorite friend." They love to be around Rick because he is the funmeister! He's loud and boisterous; he loves to tickle and play and laugh and do crazy things that bring them great delight.

Recently, at Grandparents' Day at our grandkids' elementary school, we finished visiting Kaylie's and Cassidy's classrooms and walked with them out to the playground for recess. I, ever the obedient rule follower, sat down with the other rule-following grandparents under the awning in the outdoor lunch area. Rick ran past me with our eight-year-old granddaughter, Kaylie, and six-year-old Cassidy in tow. Over his shoulder he shouted, "I'm gonna go play with the girls on the playground!" Of course, that made me nervous. *Should he be doing that? Is that against the school rules?* Within seconds, a small crowd of grade schoolers, drawn by shouts of laughter and delight, had gathered around Rick as he played a raucous game of "Red Light, Green Light" with our granddaughters. Soon, dozens of screaming boys and girls were running toward Rick when he said, "Green light," and then shrieking with mock terror as he chased them back to their safe zone during the "red light" portion of the game. Over all the ear-splitting laughter and noise, I could hear Kaylie's exuberant declaration, "My Papa always starts a party!" So true.

Kids *know*! They know when someone is fun. After Jesus gathered the children in his arms, hugged and kissed them as only God-in-flesh could do, I can only imagine the giggle-fests the children had. I wonder if sometimes he would draw a child to him and whisper in her ear, "See that tree over there? I made that tree! Isn't it the coolest tree you've ever seen?" He interacted with them in such a way that they wanted to be around him. That tells us a lot about who he was.

Not only did children love Jesus, but crowds of adults followed him everywhere, so much so that it became difficult for him to get away for private prayer.

The fact that people were around Jesus all the time doesn't mean he was a drop-dead-gorgeous hunk. In fact, the Bible tells us, "He wasn't some handsome king. Nothing about the way he looked made him attractive to us" (Isa. 53:2 CEV). Something indefinably charismatic about Jesus drew people to him; something about his demeanor and the way he interacted with people was attractive. He was someone others wanted to be around.

It's no wonder, then, that Jesus was invited to *a lot* of parties. You and I don't invite dull, boring people to parties unless we feel some sort of obligation. We try to invite people who are interesting and fun and who will add some spice and sparkle to a party.

So it's interesting to me that not only did Jesus get invited to a lot of parties, but many of his stories are based around parties. Most of them had to do with who got invited to parties and who didn't. That makes sense when we remember that Jesus enjoyed life. He was so fully engaged in these parties that some people accused him of being a glutton or a drunk.

Jesus wasn't a drunk. He was just a party guy, someone who was out there mingling with people, not sitting in a corner by a potted palm tree. And people loved it. Jesus's attitude toward life showed that he was a man of joy.

A Man of Joy through His Words

Part of rediscovering Jesus, the man of joy, involves taking a look at how he conveyed his joyful essence through his words. We don't usually think of Jesus as having a comedy act. But he told jokes! He was, in fact, hilariously funny. The very idea that Jesus told jokes and went for the laugh lines with his audience might be shocking to some of you who are used to thinking of him only as the somber and serious guy. The problem is that you and I just don't get his humor. The chasm of language, culture, and time keeps us from fully understanding Jesus's intent. Since we don't get his humor, we tend to skip right over it.

Take Luke 18:25, for example. If I asked you to read it out loud, you would probably read it in a flat, monotone voice with no particular emphasis or much of an inflection: "For it is easier for a camel to go through the eye of a needle than for a rich man to enter the kingdom of God" (NKJV). Boring! But that's the way we typically read Scripture—like we're reading the phone book! I guarantee that Jesus didn't say it like that. He was using an exaggerated word picture, a common way in Jewish culture to say something funny. His audience loved it—they thought he was a riot! They couldn't believe the funny lines that fell from his lips and the jokes he was telling.

Why did he use so much humor? The great thing about humor that's still true today is that once you get people laughing you can slide the truth in there too. You don't resist truth as much if you're laughing. So Jesus used humor to make his point, to tell truths to those who were listening who might be cautious about accepting his teaching.

I want to show you a couple other laugh lines in Jesus's teachings.

In Matthew 23:24, Jesus warns scribes and Pharisees, "Blind guides! You strain your water so you won't accidentally swallow a gnat, but you swallow a camel!" (NLT). Jesus was referring to their habit of concentrating on teeny-tiny laws concerning washing their hands and ignoring the great big laws of loving their neighbor. That's like straining out a tiny bug that you're choking on while you swallow a camel whole, according to Jesus. To us, it's not that funny; to his audience, it was great, edgy humor.

But my favorite joke from Jesus is in Matthew 7:3, 5. Jesus is talking to one of the large crowds that gathered around him on a regular basis. Evidently, he had noticed his disciples' petty arguments, because Jesus again turns to exaggeration and metaphor to say, "And why worry about a speck in your friend's eye when you have a log in your own? . . . First get rid of the log in your own eye; then you will see well enough to deal with the speck in your friend's eye" (NLT).

Try it yourself—try reading these verses to your best friend or your small group when you're together this week. Get loud! Use your hands to exaggerate the tiny speck that is in your friend's eye, and then use BIG hand motions to indicate the gigantic log that is in your own eye. I promise that you and your friends will be smiling, at the very least, if not laughing by the time you're through with your little experiment. The absurdity of getting all worked up about a small fault your friend has when you have a colossal error in your own life will become clear to you, and you will catch a glimpse of Jesus's powerful communication style. When we read these stories with new eyes, his words come alive. His relationships come alive. He becomes a real man talking to real people. A real man of joy.

A Man of Joy through His Actions

We read in John 2 that Jesus was at a wedding (another party!) in the town of Cana. It was customary to offer wine at a wedding. Now, I don't know if more people showed up than the host was expecting, but toward the end of the celebration, he ran out of wine. All he had left were jugs of water.

Mary, Jesus's mother, was there. She looked at Jesus and said, more or less, "You fix this. You can figure something out."

Jesus answered, "Why did you come to me? My time has not yet come" (John 2:4 GW).

Through the years, when I've heard this story told at church, I've imagined Jesus saying, "Mom! Would you back off? You're blowing my cover! Please just chill out and leave me alone." Jesus is harsh with her, puts her down, and tells her to mind her own business.

But now I don't believe he talked that way to her. Now that I understand Jesus more fully, I think his words sounded more like this, said in a friendly, conspiratorial whisper: "Shhhh! Mom! Thank you for believing in me. I really appreciate it! But today's not the day. It's not time yet, Mom. Thanks, but not yet."

The interesting thing to me is that Jesus went ahead and turned the water into wine—and not just a cheap grocery-store wine but an incredibly fine wine with a rich bouquet. The Bible said it was the best wine served that day.

I don't know exactly why Jesus performed his first miracle at a wedding, but I think it fits perfectly with his joyful essence to choose a festive social event to unveil his public ministry. I think that says something vitally important about him.

Another story that reflects Jesus as a man of joy is in Matthew 14. Jesus has been ministering to thousands of people for hours, and he can't escape the crowds. Greatly in need of some peace and quiet, he tells his disciples to get in a boat and go to the other side of the lake while he goes up on a mountainside to pray.

In the middle of the night, the disciples are startled— scared spitless, actually—to see Jesus gliding across the water to them. The Bible says they screamed in their terror, thinking Jesus was a ghost. Before we put them down for their fear, it's good to remember that no one had ever seen someone walk on water before.

Jesus tries to calm them down by identifying himself and urges them to not be afraid. Evidently, Peter is quick to accept that the water-walking apparition is Jesus because he calls out, "Jesus? Is that really you? If so, tell me to come to you on the water."

Jesus says, "It's me, Peter. Come on down!"

Peter hops out of the boat and starts walking on the water toward Jesus. Jesus is smiling at him, expecting him to come.

All of a sudden, Peter's focus on walking on the water is broken as a chilly breeze off the lake pulls at his long robes and the precarious nature of his adventure hits him like a ton of bricks: *I'm walking on water!* He looks down, and the minute he looks down, he starts to sink. "Lord, save me!" he screams. Matthew 14:31 says, "Immediately Jesus reached out his hand and caught him. 'You of little faith,' he said, 'why did you doubt?'"

My entire life I've heard that verse read in a tone of voice that conveys condemnation: "Peter! How many times have I told you I would take care of you? Give me your hand—right now. Get up here, you of little faith."

I don't believe that anymore. God does not criticize us or put us down when we take baby steps of faith. Peter *was* taking steps of faith when he got out of the boat. God knew he needed encouragement, not disapproval.

I believe that Jesus looked at Peter with tenderness in his eyes, pulled Peter close to him, and said, "Peter, Peter! Oh, you of little faith. Why did you doubt me? I told you I'd take care of you. I'm here for you." That's the way God reacts to us when we mess up in our attempts to serve him.

In another story in Matthew 14, the Bible says that five thousand people heard that Jesus was in town and came to him seeking healing for their sick. The number in the crowd was probably closer to fifteen thousand because you have to figure the men brought their wives, who brought their children.

As it got close to evening, the disciples began to be concerned about feeding the mass of people who didn't seem to be in a hurry to go home. They strategized among themselves and figured the best plan was for Jesus to tell the crowd to disperse and go find food on their own. They had their speech all memorized and thought Jesus would applaud their organizational skills. However, Jesus threw them a huge curveball when he responded to their plan with these words in verse 16: "They do not need to go away. You give them something to eat."

What did he expect them to do? The disciples couldn't feed fifty people, let alone fifteen thousand! But he looked at them and said, "You feed them."

Again, we're so used to glossing over familiar passages of Scripture that we miss the punch of the story, and our dry, listless way of reading it out loud just compounds the problem. Jesus didn't turn to his disciples and say, "You guys blew it again! I put you in charge of the lunch, and what did you do? You didn't even count all the women and the children. I can't ever depend on you to take care of things. I have to do it myself around here."

That wasn't the way it was. He took that moment to show them that while they were inadequate to take care of the need of the moment, they didn't need to worry. He would take care of them, and he did. He took a little boy's lunch of fish and loaves and he broke it and he multiplied it and he fed all those people. And there was so much left over, the Bible says, that the extra food filled twelve baskets. Jesus took care of his followers. He didn't put his disciples down as they were trying to figure out how to do what he asked them to do.

Friends, Jesus was a man of joy. *He was a man of joy!* He showed it in his attitude; he drew crowds who couldn't get enough of him. He showed it in his words; he was a master communicator who impacted those who listened to him in person two thousand years ago, and he impacts us today. He showed joy in his actions; he treated people with good humor and patient understanding of their human foibles, and he was skillful in bringing them to the spiritual realizations they needed.

His joyful essence was evidenced particularly in the way he interacted with his disciples. He spent three years with them, day in and day out. He did not spend those three years with them as a lecturer on the speaking circuit who used them to organize his comings and goings: "Okay, let's go over the agenda. Who will be taking care of the donkey this afternoon? Oh, and make sure the people know that I'm coming." He didn't relate as a distant professor who made them sit still while he instilled: "Now, I have three points I want to make today, and I'll be testing you later. Is everybody writing down what I'm saying?"

No, Jesus lived his life with them. They saw him when he was sweaty and stinky from a long walk from village to village. They knew when his stomach growled from hunger pains. They probably heard him pass gas and burp a few dozen times. I'm not saying that to be sensational; I really believe it. Jesus spent nearly every waking—and sleeping—hour with these twelve men for three years. How could they not really *know* each other? I'm sure Jesus and his friends shared many private jokes, funny stories, and poignant memories, which happens only when people spend intentional time together. I am convinced they laughed till their sides hurt at every opportunity. He loved them and invested in their lives as individuals. I think he probably knew the names of their family members for a couple of generations back; he knew the beauty and dysfunction that created each one of them. He believed in them, ultimately entrusting them with his gospel message of a joyous relationship with God. As his time on earth drew to a close, they were the ones he wanted near him—these friends who had become brothers.

Joy in a World of Sorrow

Why does it matter that Jesus was a man of joy? It matters so much more than you might have ever realized! Some of you may need permission to seek a life of joy for yourself. The burden of grief that you carry, the health issues, the relational pain, the financial questions, the internal struggles and temptations no one else knows about—sometimes all of that weighs you down so much that you give up on the idea of joy. At times I have felt I could identify with the title given to Jesus in Isaiah; I could call myself "Kay Warren, woman of sorrows." Perhaps that title fits you today as well, and you could fill in your name too. Many of us need permission to recognize sorrow but go beyond it and still choose a life of joy.

Yes, Jesus suffered, but we can't stop there. We can't let that truth dominate how we act and how we speak about him. There was a *reason* why Jesus chose to endure all that he did. There was a reason why he allowed himself to be bloodied and beaten and tortured. Hebrews 12:2 gives us an insider, behind-the-scenes look at why Jesus allowed all of that to happen: "who for the joy set before him endured the cross."

But what was the joy that was set before him? What joy was so rich, so satisfying, so deep that he was willing to suffer such terrible abuse? *You* were the joy set before him! *I* was the joy set before him! He suffered so he could be reconciled with *you*. With *me*. When people spat at him, his disciples left him, and everyone mocked him, he was thinking of the joy. When he was flogged, when that cruel crown of thorns was jammed on his head, and when he hung on the cross, he got through it because he was holding on to the joy of presenting us to God.

> *What joy was so rich, so satisfying, so deep that he was willing to suffer such terrible abuse? You were the joy set before him!*

Here she is, Father; I brought her back to you. The joy of restoring the broken relationship, of living with me and you forever . . . that was the joy set before him, that was the joy that kept him nailed to the cross.

Jesus knew that for him to fulfill his God-given role here on earth, he would have to experience abandonment, betrayal, torture, and death. Yet knowing full well what was ahead of him, he chose to laugh, to tell jokes, to roll around on the ground with children, to build rich relationships, to have meaningful work, to experience joy.

Jesus's life is an illustration of the two train tracks converging into one. He shows us how to see joy, a joy that sometimes comes in darkness. And for that joy he endured the greatest suffering anyone has known.

This is what Jesus's life tells me: It is possible to experience enormous burdens, pain, and struggles—the weight of the world on our frail shoulders—and still experience joy. Jesus's life reminds me that joy is possible no matter what. His life gives me permission to seek a life of joy for myself even in a world of sorrow.

—— **PRAYER** ——

Thank you for showing me, Jesus, who you are, that you are a full-of-joy kind of Savior. Jesus, I thank you that when you were dying on the cross, you held out the joy of being reunited with me. Because of that joy, you allowed yourself to be tortured and killed. Because of that joy, you made a way for me to come into relationship with you. Thank you that you carried my sin, my rebellion. Thank you that your life shows me how to live. Thank you for showing me that even in sorrow I can know blessings and joy and laughter. Teach me what it means to choose joy. In the name of Jesus, man of joy, I pray. Amen.

FOR REFLECTION AND APPLICATION

1. Reread Jesus's words, looking for humor. Give yourself permission to laugh at the metaphors he uses!

2. Imagine Jesus—a man of sorrows and joy—walking through life with you today. What would he laugh with you about? What would he cry with you about?

JOY Is A CONVICTION OF MY MIND

PART 2

Discovering a New Way of Thinking

Early in my marriage, I wasn't very skilled at resolving conflict. When Rick and I would have a disagreement and my feelings would get hurt, I found myself resistant to reconnecting with him, even if he was ready to resolve things. I waited for my negative feelings to dissipate so that we could be close again, but hours would pass and the negative feelings would remain. I didn't understand why I couldn't make my feelings cooperate, and I repeated the same pattern, argument after argument.

Finally, someone shared with me a principle that altered our relationship: What we think determines how we act, and how we act determines how we feel. I was operating on the belief that I needed to *feel* differently before I could *think* differently. But the formula is reversed: Our thinking changes first, our actions come next, and our feelings follow. Instead of waiting for my feelings to change so I could act in a forgiving way, I needed to change my thoughts. Instead of rehearsing the argument, I needed to rehearse God's Word in my mind. Once my thoughts were back on track and in harmony with God's instructions about relationships, I could make the right choices whether I felt like it or not. Rick has said many times, "You can't feel your way into an action, but you can act your way into a feeling."

That's why it's good that joy is much more than a feeling. The Bible says in Philippians 4:4, "Always be full of joy in the Lord. I say it again—rejoice!" (NLT). You can't command a feeling, but you can command a thought and an action. God tells us how we must think and how we must behave, knowing that our feelings will always be the last to fall in line.

As we've already discussed, joy is a *settled assurance* about God, a *quiet confidence* in God, and a *determined choice* to praise God. To have this settled assurance, we must hold convictions about who God is. We must have right thinking about him.

We looked at James 1:2–4 in chapter 2, but it's worth looking at again:

> *Consider* it a sheer gift, friends, when tests and challenges come at you from all sides. You *know* that under pressure, your faith-life is forced into the open and shows its true colors. So don't try to get out of anything prematurely. Let it do its work so you become mature and well-developed, not deficient in any way. (Message)

Other translations say to "*count* it all joy" when you face hardship. Some say to "*consider* it a great opportunity for joy when trials and troubles come your way." *Consider. Count. Know.* Those are words that have to do with our mind. How we think. The way we look at a situation.

This passage of Scripture tells us that joy begins in the mind. As we'll see later in the book, joy also has to do with our heart, our emotions, and our attitude. Ultimately, joy comes down to something that we *do*. But joy starts with a new way of thinking that changes how we respond to trials in our lives.

As we see God as he really is, a fundamental shift happens in our view of life. That's what this section is about.

FOUR

Drinking from Dry Wells

This is what the Almighty LORD, the Holy One of Israel, says: "You can be saved by returning to me. You can have rest. You can be strong by being quiet and by trusting me. But you don't want that."

Isaiah 30:15 GW

What does not satisfy when we find it was not the thing we were desiring.

C. S. Lewis

Consider this: What if the things you think will give you joy really won't? What if you're looking for satisfaction in all the wrong places, but you don't believe it?

The Bible tells us that joy is available to all of us—and yet joy eludes many. In desperation, we try anything and everything we think might hold out the possibility of quenching the thirst for joy. We look to people. We look to the place where we live or where we want to live. We look to our possessions, our position, and our personality.

These things may give you happiness for a time, but eventually they will fail you, because as we've already said, happiness isn't enough. It never is. What we've counted on to establish joy in our lives isn't sufficient.

Imagine this scene with me. You're walking in the desert in the searing heat; you've been walking in circles for days, and you're pretty sure you're lost. Your thirst is overwhelming because you have no water, and if you don't find some very quickly, you will die. Then you see in the distance something that looks like a lemonade stand. It has a flashing neon sign that advertises "Living Water Available Here!" God is behind the stand, holding out a glass of clear, ice-cold water to you. You stumble up to the stand, barely able to walk, and you say to him, "Thanks, God! I see that lovely glass of water in your hand, and I really appreciate your offer. But if you don't mind, I'm going to grab the shovel I see lying on the ground and I'm going to dig my own cistern." So you pick up the shovel and begin to dig. And with a lot of effort, you manage to create a cistern that holds water. But very soon it develops cracks and runs dry, and you are thirsty again. All the while God waits patiently, holding out the cool, refreshing liquid that promises relief for your desperate thirst.

Does that scenario ring any bells for you? That could be the story of my search for joy: thirsty, longing for relief, ignoring God's invitation, choosing to search desperately on my own, coming up dry.

Of course, we're not the first people to look for joy in all the wrong places. Centuries ago, the Israelites forgot that God was the source of their redemption. They turned to the false gods the surrounding nations worshiped rather than to the God who had led them out of Egypt.

Through the prophet Jeremiah, God tells the Israelites, "My people have committed two sins: They have forsaken me, the spring of living water, and have dug their own cisterns, broken cisterns that cannot hold water" (Jer. 2:13).

Here Jeremiah uses language that his listeners would readily understand. "Living water" refers to the running water of springs that never stop. In Israel at that time, springs provided the most dependable, refreshing, cool, clear water available. Cisterns, by contrast, were large pits dug into rocks that were used to collect rainwater. Not only was the water in cisterns dirty, but it could also easily run out if the rains were light that year. Cisterns were also undependable—if a cistern had a crack, it would not hold water at all.

It didn't make any sense to choose a cistern over a spring. Yet that is what the nation of Israel was doing when it abandoned Yahweh, their God, to pursue false gods.

Just like the Israelites, we—instead of going to God for satisfaction in life—get our shovels and start digging our own cisterns. We believe that our cisterns will hold enough water to quench our thirsty souls. Then we go to those cisterns when we don't have enough joy in our lives, hoping they will produce joy for us.

The problem is that the cisterns you and I dig don't hold enough water to get us through the tough times. They crack and run dry. Rather than turning to God, we just dig a little harder. We drag ourselves out day after day looking for joy in the same place that didn't bring joy the day before.

Larry Crabb says:

> People are moving in wrong directions in response to their thirst. They refuse to trust God to look after their thirst. Instead, they insist on maintaining control of finding their own satisfaction. They're all moving about determined to satisfy the longings of their hearts by picking up a shovel, looking for a likely spot to dig, and then searching for a fulfillment they can generate. To put it simply, people want to run their own lives. Fallen man is both terrified of vulnerability and committed to maintaining independence.[1]

Let me show you how this has worked in my life more than once. I can think of a dozen times when I've had a bad day. A situation is breaking my heart. I'm upset, lonely, scared, and anxious. I think, *I've got to talk to somebody. Rick's busy. I'll call my friend. She'll listen to me.* And I dial the number of a friend. She listens and gives me great advice. She even prays with me. She shares the Word of God with me. It helps for a moment. But after I hang up, I find myself feeling anxious again. I'm still thirsty.

I decide I need to distract myself. I turn on music I really like. It works for a little while. My mood lightens a bit. But then I remember why I was feeling anxious. I'm thirsty again.

Food! Food will help! So I start foraging through the refrigerator. I find last night's roast and potatoes and carrots, and it all tastes so good. But I'm still thirsty. *Chips! Chips and salsa! Chips and guacamole! Chips and ANYTHING will fix what's bothering me.*

After a few minutes of mass chip consumption, I've got a stomachache, but I remain anxious. Still stubbornly focused on alleviating my thirst, I think, *Chocolate! Nothing can stand in the way of chocolate.* So I get out my stash of candy.

But within minutes I'm feeling that familiar ache again. God, why am I still so thirsty? I'm stuffed! I've talked to a friend. I've distracted myself. So why am I still thirsty? And by the way, why won't you help me? I am trying my hardest to be joyful, and I can't understand why you stand there and do nothing.

I've been trying to dig my own cistern. I've picked up shovel after shovel after shovel in my attempts to find joy. And clueless to the fact that God will *never* help me dig my own cisterns, I get bitter and angry at God.

God may use other things and people in our lives to give us water. But he won't help us dig our own cisterns. Not because he's mean, but because he knows that the cisterns we dig will leave us thirsty and dry. He puts his efforts into drawing us back to himself, back to the living water he offers.

Author and pastor M. Craig Barnes writes, "Don't expect Jesus to save us by teaching us to depend on the things we are afraid of losing. . . . He will abandon every crusade that searches for salvation from anything or anyone other than God."[2]

So let's take a closer look at the broken cisterns—false sources of joy—most of us go to in our search for lasting joy.

Looking for Love: People

My primary false source of joy is people: my husband, my children, my friends, the people I'm in ministry with. I consistently look to them to provide joy. When they're happy with me, I'm happy. When they're unhappy with me, I'm unhappy. I'm sad to say that my joy level goes up and down based almost entirely on the people in my life.

My husband is my most important go-to guy for joy. Rick's a very emotional man, and his emotions flit across his face sometimes when he's not even aware of it. I'm always trying to interpret those expressions and determine if they have anything to do with me. *Does that look mean he's mad at me? What did that sigh mean? I know he said one thing, but did he mean something else?* I'm constantly evaluating the poor guy!

Occasionally, when Rick comes home from work after a very hard and stressful day, all he wants to do is plop down on the couch, read his newspaper, and watch a little bit of television before dinner. He's not always that interested in the fact that I am eagerly waiting to tell him all about *my* day—especially when he first walks in the door. If I'm not careful, I decide that his mood has to do with me more than it has to do with him just being tired. I find my joy sinking because it is tied into what he does, what he says, and how he seems to be feeling.

I've realized that my level of joy is tied to my expectations of my spouse—and I have a lot of expectations! My first expectation is that when I talk to Rick, he will listen to me. That's fair, right? (I happen to know I'm not the only one who wants this.) And not only do I expect him to listen, but I also expect him to figure out what I mean. On top of that, I expect him to figure it out *without my having to explain it.* He should know me so well that he will understand exactly what I mean and what I intended to say even if I didn't say it. I expect him to know that all the time in every conversation, no matter what else is going on in his life! And when he doesn't meet my "reasonable" expectations, my joy diminishes. In fact, it tanks. You know what I'm talking about, don't you?

I have also realized that sometimes I have had high expectations of finding joy through my kids. Let's be honest. We want gratitude. We want satisfaction. We have this totally unrealistic dream in our minds. We envision walking into our kids' room, telling them to clean it up, and having them respond, "Oh, thank you so much. Thank you for caring about my character. Thank you for desiring that I grow up to be a responsible adult. I will *gladly* clean my room AND do the dishes AND come home on time. I will do it with no complaining, just for you, O great parent of mine!" We keep waiting to hear those words so we can be joyful. Has it ever happened that way for you? No? Me neither.

God may use other things and people in our lives to give us water. But he won't help us dig our own cisterns.

The truth is that I have occasionally looked at my kids and thought, Let's get this straight. You owe me! I gave you life! I birthed you and lost my gorgeous figure over you! You're the reason that everything sags and hangs down to my knees! You owe me big-time!

Even more significantly, we might think in a secret part of our mind, This wasn't what I expected parenting to be. I was counting on a healthy child, not a son who has autism. I was counting on a child to soak up my love when I adopted her, not a daughter who rejects me. I thought having kids running around the kitchen at dinnertime would be fulfilling, not make me want to scream!

When will we figure it out? Our children are not here to meet our need for appreciation. They were not born to meet *our* expectations for their lives. They are here to fulfill God's purpose for them (Ps. 138:8).

Yet day after day we look to our children or our spouses or our friends or our co-workers to fulfill us. When they don't, we get angry. They owe us! That's when most of us pick up our weapons of choice. I'm not proud of the weapons I have been known to use when I'm wounded, but I will be honest and share mine with you as long as you will think truthfully about yours. My favorite weapon when I'm disappointed in someone is either the cold shoulder (the not-so-subtle way of turning away from the offending person) or a sarcastic comment that cuts like a knife.

As we hold our weapon of choice, we justify our attitude. We decide that if the other person would just change, we would be joyful.

Why is this? Because we're expecting the people in our lives to meet needs they cannot meet. They were never supposed to.

Just Click Your Heels Together: Places

When Rick and I got married, we rented an apartment in a new complex that offered tenants the choice of units with a lime green, baby blue, or dark brown color theme. The carpet, wallpaper, and one wall in each room echoed the color theme. Don't ask me why—maybe because it was the mid-70s and we were still in our psychedelic hippie days—but we chose the lime green unit. What initially seemed fresh and hip and funky quickly became nauseating! I couldn't escape the fluorescent lime green on nearly every surface of our small apartment. "What were we thinking? Why didn't we go for the baby blue?" I moaned to Rick. "I will never live in a place with lime green carpet again!" Wouldn't you know it—our next two apartments had lime green carpet! Like I said, it must have been a 70s thing.

I'll bet I'm not the only one to regret a choice I made about where I live. I imagine you have said something like this before:

In my next house I'll have more storage.

We should have bought that other model.

I should have rented something closer to the office.

If only we lived closer to my parents.

If only we didn't live so close to your parents.

How often do you catch yourself dreaming of the next place you'll live? For many of us, our house, city, and neighborhood carry a lot of weight. The trouble is that we can move to a new house, a new city, or a new neighborhood and one thing stays the same: us! Our needs and expectations move with us.

No matter where we live, we are tempted to compare our home to others. We're satisfied until we go to the Christmas party in a house bigger, better decorated, or newer than ours. We find ourselves thinking, *If I lived in that house, the parties I would throw! The people I would welcome! The ministry I could do if only I lived there instead of here!* All the potential and goodness of our own home are gone. Our joy goes with them.

There Your Heart Will Be Also: Possessions

The Bible is clear about the deceptiveness of attaining possessions as a means to finding joy (Matt. 13:22), and it tells us repeatedly that the acquisition of material things can be a trap. Luke 12:15 says, "Beware! Guard against every kind of greed. Life is not measured by how much you own" (NLT). Jesus lays it out in no uncertain terms in Matthew 6:19–21: "Don't store up treasures here on earth, where moths eat them and rust destroys them, and where thieves break in and steal. Store your treasures in heaven, where moths and rust cannot destroy, and thieves do not break in and steal. Wherever your treasure is, there the desires of your heart will also be" (NLT).

Not only is the pursuit of wealth as a means to lasting joy a waste of time and an irrefutable way to measure what we really value, but the Bible also tells us that always wanting just a little bit more causes us to become jealous and envious of others who have greater financial and material success than we do.

The Bible says that envy rots the bones (Prov. 14:30). Envy has only one outcome in our lives: discontent. And discontent worms its way into the center of who we are, into the marrow that should produce health, and destroys us from the inside out. Discontent is ugly, and it turns us into sour, bitter people.

Do you remember how happy you were as a little kid on Christmas morning, thoroughly jazzed by a new toy, until you went next door to show off your loot to your best friend only to see that they had even more? Suddenly your present looked lonely. Rather than being happy for your friend's good fortune, all your pleasure evaporated in seconds as envy settled in. Somebody should have warned us then that it would only get worse as we got older and the toys grew more sophisticated.

Now we imagine that if we just had "that one thing" we would have more joy. I've had that car for ten years, and it's high time I replaced it. Maybe if I had a new car I would actually get to the gym in the morning. Maybe a new car would change everything for me. And if I had a newer television, one with a bigger screen, or a new computer, maybe that would make a real difference in my life too. That's what's wrong. I don't have a new [fill in the blank].

This is why the Bible has such strong words of caution about valuing money and material possessions over people and relationships. God knows doing so has the power to strip us of joy.

Instead, we can model ourselves after the apostle Paul's example. Many of you have memorized Philippians 4:13, "I can do all things through Him who strengthens me" (NASB), but have no clue about the context of that verse. Paul has been telling his friends at Philippi not to be alarmed about his financial needs because "I have learned to be content whatever the circumstances. I know what it is to be in need, and I know what it is to have plenty. I have learned the secret of being content in any and every situation, whether well fed or hungry, whether living in plenty or in want" (Phil. 4:11–12). After reassuring them that he can do just fine with a little or a lot, *then* he tells them how: through Christ, who gives him strength.

Paul says, "Don't worry about me; I have figured out how to have joy—be content—when times are fantastic and when times are terrible. Either way, I find contentment through the power of Jesus Christ. When I have a lot, I remind myself that earthly riches are fleeting and refuse to greedily seek more. When I am in need, I remind myself that earthly riches cannot define my worth; God will take care of me. I face life through the power I receive from my Savior, Jesus."

No wonder Paul lived with joy; he found his strength in Jesus, not in possessions.

Lonely at the Top: Position

There's a hierarchy—spoken or unspoken—in every church, every job, every organization. We're happy as long as we like where we are in the hierarchy. But whoa! Let someone receive credit for *your* idea, get the promotion you thought was yours, make more money than you do even though you work twice as hard, and happiness goes out the window.

Soon you begin to think you'd be a lot happier on the next rung up. You begin to plot how to make your move on the co-worker who holds the job you want. To make it worse, it's tempting to start looking over your shoulder to see who is climbing up the ladder behind you, ready to push you out of your spot.

Striving for a different position or title is not wrong. But joy will not survive in an environment of suspicion, greed, or resentment, because every one of those reactions suggests dependence on a homemade cistern. They imply that a new position or greater recognition will bring more joy than what you have now. And that's an idea that won't hold water.

It's Not You, It's Me: Personality

The last false source of joy is the one I think we go to on a daily basis without being aware of it: our personality. We firmly believe that extroverts have a jump start on the rest of us when it comes to joy. They were standing first in line when God gave out joy, so they're happier with life. We think that if we don't have the right personality for joy, we're just not cut out for it, as if joy is available only to a certain kind of person.

I was watching a Winnie the Pooh cartoon with my kids years ago when I thought to myself, *Rick is just like Tigger!* That humorous idea launched me into a silly habit of assigning labels to other people I love, and before I knew it, the "Winnie the Pooh School of Personalities" was born. Of course, it's not scientific, and if you really want to study personalities, there's no lack of scholarly information available. This is just a simple approach to the four basic personality types in a lighthearted way.

Let's look at Winnie the Pooh first. Pooh doesn't get too worked up about much of anything except his drive to find honey. He's pretty carefree, middle of the road in his emotional responses, and doesn't quite understand why others get so emotional about everything! If you have a friend who is an easygoing Winnie the Pooh, she will likely have a very hard time making decisions. If you say to her, "Why don't you choose where we're going for lunch today?" she will probably say, "Oh, I don't care—why don't YOU choose?" If you insist, "No, you decide this time—I've chosen the restaurant the last three times," she'll likely squirm and demur with, "Oh, I really don't care; you choose." At this point, you're probably ready to throttle her cute little Pooh neck! But we need Winnie the Pooh friends because they remain steady and sure when the rest of us are spinning wildly out of control.

Then there's Rabbit. Rabbits are goal-oriented; they want the garden planted right, and they want it planted right *now*. Rabbits are the task-oriented high achievers and the ones who get things done in life. Every committee needs a few Rabbits because they will cross all the t's and dot all the i's—the event will be organized well! But your Rabbit friend probably isn't the one you want to go to for comfort or encouragement if you're having a bad day. Rabbits are not known for their high empathy quotient. They will probably listen impatiently to your sad saga and say, "Buck up! Life is hard! You just gotta get back in there and keep trying!" But we need Rabbits. The world would be in a shambles without them. Nothing would ever get done without Rabbits who strategize and make dreams a reality.

Tiggers are the extroverts. They're the bouncy, trouncy, flouncy, pouncy, fun-fun-fun-fun-fun personalities. They walk into a room and suck all the oxygen out of it by the force of their personality. They tell stories with great enthusiasm and go into elaborate detail—even if the details get a little muddy along the way. They can't remember your name but enthusiastically tell others you're one of their best friends. Tiggers may forget they were supposed to meet you for lunch, but they're so much fun when they finally arrive that you forgive them! No matter how much they irritate us at times, we need Tiggers to brighten our days!

Then there's my favorite because it's me: Eeyore. Eeyores are creative, intense, perfectionistic and *feeeel* things very deeply. They tend to be pessimistic and even gloomy at times, but often that's because Eeyores carry the pain and sorrow of the world on their shoulders. Sometimes they're not much fun to be around! But if you want a creative idea, an in-depth conversation, or an empathetic ear, call your Eeyore friend. Eeyores add a rich dimension to relationships and conversations because they have such depth and breadth of emotion and are able to pull the rich emotions out of others as well. The world would be a shallow, cold, uncaring place without Eeyores.

It's easy to look at one of the other personalities and say, *I could be joyful if I were like Tigger! I could be joyful if I were as carefree as Winnie the Pooh. Of course I could.* But here's what we need to be aware of. Each personality type has strengths AND weaknesses. Just because your friend is an extroverted Tigger doesn't mean they understand joy. Tiggers have dangers too. They tend to depend on the force of their personality and not the Spirit of God. Why do they need God when they've got their personality? And sometimes Tiggers get so used to the sensation of being "up" that when they hit a wall emotionally, it is likely to be very confusing and disorienting to them; they don't know what to do with low emotions.

Those who are Rabbits can find joy in completing their tasks and checking items off their to-do list instead of in God. Accomplishing tasks can become a substitute for a meaningful walk with God. Winnie the Poohs can be a little smug and take great pride in the fact that while the rest of us are spinning like crazy tops, they're walking calmly through life. Why would Winnie the Pooh need God for joy? With a relaxed attitude, shouldn't everyone be able to experience joy? Eeyores probably face the greatest challenge of all the personalities when it comes to choosing joy because their natural bent is toward introspection, pessimism, and perfectionism.

Here is the foundational truth that each of us needs to remember: God is the only true source of joy.

But no personality has either an edge or an excuse when it comes to experiencing joy. The Lord recently told me, "Kay, I want you to stop using your personality as an excuse for not experiencing joy on a daily basis; you've become a prisoner of your personality. I want you—a naturally gloomy little Eeyore—to experience joy." Have you discovered this about yourself yet? Can you see how easy it is to become a prisoner of your personality type? Over time we can develop more loyalty to our personality than we have to God and his command to choose joy. I will always be an Eeyore. You will always be a Tigger, or a Rabbit, or a Winnie the Pooh—but we don't need to hide behind our personalities or rely on them to determine the level of joy we experience in life.

True joy—apart from our emotions or human inclinations—is possible. Joy is a gift of the Holy Spirit intended for all personalities at all times.

Still Thirsty

Let's just admit it because we've all done it more times than we can count. We've expected people, places, possessions, positions, and personalities to give us joy. They have given us short-term happiness but left us gasping for water. Desperate for relief, most of us have made some pretty serious attempts at digging our own cisterns. Doing so has left some of us exhausted, to the point of despair, even hopelessness.

God says, "It's okay; that's what's supposed to happen." *What? God wants me to experience despair?* Only to bring you face-to-face with how utterly inadequate you are at providing water for yourself and to point the way to himself, the only true source of joy.

Here is the foundational truth that each of us needs to remember: *God is the only true source of joy.* God will be there when all else is shaking. He will be there when the people you love let you down or leave you or die. He will be there when the place you thought would make you happy doesn't satisfy any longer. He will be there when the possession is lost or gets broken. He will be there when your position changes or is given to someone else. He will be there when your personality just isn't enough.

He is the spring of living water that will never run dry. That's what we're going to look at in the next chapter.

—— **PRAYER** ——

Father, you know I am dry and empty. Yet I have been digging wells to try to find water. I have looked to people, places, positions, and possessions for lasting joy. I have tried to hide behind my personality. God, these are broken cisterns that will always disappoint me. Forgive me for forsaking you, the spring of living water. Forgive me for looking anywhere else for true fulfillment. Help me to turn to you first for satisfaction. In the name of Jesus, amen.

FOR REFLECTION AND APPLICATION

1. What false sources of joy trap you? Is it people, places, possessions, positions, or personality?

2. Where do you fit in the "Winnie the Pooh School of Personalities"? How do you think that affects your ability to find joy?

FIVE

Adopting Heaven's
Value System

There I will go to the altar of God,
to God—the source of all my joy.
Psalm 43:4 NLT

To embrace God's point of view, however briefly, is to be joyful.

Mike Mason

As we've seen, life is like a set of train tracks. The track of joy and the track of sorrow run side by side, inseparably, throughout our lives. We are constantly experiencing both joy and sorrow at the same time. Some days we're able to do as James commands—consider trials a "sheer gift," an opportunity for great joy—but other days that's a tough instruction to obey.

Troubles come for all of us; whether Christian or non-Christian, no one is immune. The pesky track of hardship, struggle, and sorrow is ever present, and there are days when all we can see is what's broken, what's missing, what's lost. We write the story of our lives with possible outcomes in our minds and then replay them over and over. We ask ourselves, *What if this happens? What if that doesn't happen? What if this never changes?* Soon we can't think of anything to praise God for.

I often find myself asking, *What have you done for me lately, God? I know you blessed me in the past, but what about now? What will you do for me today?* Maybe you don't feel particularly joyful, and if you're basing your experience of joy on the presence of upbeat feelings, you can quickly forget that God is still the powerful, faithful God he's always been.

No matter how we *feel*, God, the spring of living water, never changes. That's why we need to saturate our minds with his truths. Joy begins with our convictions about spiritual truths we're willing to bet our lives on, truths that are lodged so deep within us that they produce a settled assurance about God. The more we know and understand God, the more easily we recognize that the "joy of the LORD" is our only true strength (Neh. 8:10).

Many of you might agree—Yes, I'd like to get better acquainted with God; I'd like to know how to saturate my mind with his truths, but I don't know how to do it.

Through the centuries, Christians have become intimately acquainted with God by spending time with him every day in meditation. When I say "meditation," I don't mean for you to put your mind in neutral and mindlessly sit and breathe. There is a time and a place to relax and let your mind be quiet and at rest. But meditating on God is active rather than passive. The word *meditate* means to contemplate, ponder, think, consider, reflect, or ruminate.

Just in case you've forgotten, rumination is what cows do. They chew their cud, swallow it, burp it back up, and do it all again. Cows go through this process three times! They do this to extract the maximum benefits from their cud for proper digestion and nutrition. The old saying "Contented as a cow chewing her cud" is based on fact: Cows that ruminate are happier than those that don't!

For Christians, meditation is simply "thought rumination," to ponder a thought or an idea over and over and over again. Some of you might be thinking, *I can't do that—my brain's too tired.* But as Rick says, if you can worry, you can meditate! When we're meditating on God, we're putting our brains to work rather than putting them on the shelf. Meditation is an energetic, intentional way of fully engaging our minds.

Meditating on God allows us to immerse ourselves in knowledge about him so that the joy of who he is becomes a conviction of our minds. When trials come into our lives, we will have grown to know God so intimately that we won't lose hold of joy. Saint Padre Pio stated, "Through the study of books one seeks God; by meditation one finds him."[1]

So how do you meditate on God? Meditating on God can include journaling about a particular verse, listening to life-giving music about God's character, writing down attributes of God on index cards and taping them to your bathroom mirror or keeping them in your purse for quick reference. Let me suggest five unchanging attributes of God to launch you on a lifelong pursuit of getting to know the Giver of thirst-quenching living water.

God's Worth Is Incomparable

The majesty, magnificence, and might of God are far beyond description. No human language has words that are adequate to articulate *who he is*. He exists beyond the reach of time and space and inhabits eternity. Poets, artists, composers, and authors all attempt to put words and pictures around this awesome God, but even their best efforts fall woefully short. Psalm 148:13 says, "Let them praise the name of GOD—it's the only Name worth praising. His radiance exceeds anything in earth and sky" (Message). "His radiance exceeds ANYTHING in earth and sky." Isn't that a relief? We praise God because he is bigger than we can understand.

A few years ago, I was struggling with a relational problem that seemed insurmountable, and there were many days I could not find a peaceful, joyful place within me. I live near the Pacific Ocean, and on my way home from driving my kids to school, I would frequently drive to the beach and park on a cliff above the ocean. One day in particular as I was weeping tears of hopelessness, I was struck by the sight and sound of the waters that roared and crashed on the rocks below me. Then I stared out to sea and found comfort, not in the vast, impersonal body of water but in the knowledge that the God who created the awesome waters was even bigger, grander, and more powerful than all the oceans on planet Earth combined. If he was big enough—theologians call it transcendence—to create the oceans, cause them to ebb and flow in a highly structured, organized fashion every single day, and sustain the life that is within them, then surely he was big enough to know how to handle the relational rift that was breaking my heart.

God uses dark times in our lives to reveal his majesty, to show us that he is the Creator, the Sustainer, the Deliverer, the Redeemer. He is the Almighty, the everlasting one, the source of life. He is above us. He is the one we can run to. Meditating on the measure of his worth shifts our attention away from the seemingly insurmountable circumstances we are facing to a God who transcends them all.

God's Word Is Reliable

Because Rick and I have been in the media a lot in the last few years, I've had the opportunity to see up close and personal just how mixed up a story can get! It seems like no matter how careful we are to give a reporter the correct facts, somehow the details are wrong in the final article. It's not that I think reporters are intentionally misleading or have a bias that affects their writing; I just recognize they have a difficult job. That has made me cynical about every story or news report I read, because I know they are often not completely accurate.

The Bible isn't like that. It is completely accurate, reliable, and trustworthy. Knowing that, I can be assured that when I read God's Word, I'm getting the truth—a foundation I can build my life on. Since the only thing that's completely true is God's Word, that's what we need to base our joy on. His words should be the most familiar words we know.

Not only is God a God of joy, but God's Word to us is also a Word of joy. But wouldn't you agree that most people think the Bible is a book of rules and regulations? They have the idea that if they pick up the Bible, everything they read will be a condemnation telling them what they're doing wrong and how they're failing. They see it as a book of negativity, a book of doom and gloom.

Now, here's something for you trivia buffs. In the New International Version of the Bible, there are 545 references to joy and merriment and happiness and laughing and rejoicing. That's a pretty good chunk of verses that talk about joy. You might assume there are at least that many verses that talk about sorrow and pain and tears and suffering, right? One hundred fifty-eight. One hundred fifty-eight verses talk about sorrow. Doesn't that blow your mind? There are more than three times as many verses about joy in the Bible than about sadness. The Bible is a book of joy!

Not only is God a God of joy, but God's Word to us is also a Word of joy.

And that's why one of the best ways to meditate on God's character is to read and memorize biblical truths about him. More than once in my own life I have found bits of Bible verses coming to me just when I needed a reminder of God's character.

In September 2003, I had an appointment with a radiologist for a biopsy because I'd had a suspicious mammogram recently. But I'd been told the lump in my breast was probably nothing. I went that day thinking this was just something to get out of the way, a step to rule out any problems. I had a flight scheduled for later that day to go see my father in another state for his birthday.

As I lay on the radiologist's table and that doctor casually said, "Almost certainly cancer," I was shocked.

"What?"

"Yeah, see this tumor? This is most likely cancer." And he walked out of the room.

My brain froze. I wanted to scream and I wanted to cry and I wanted to do everything all at once. In that moment of being left alone to deal with the words nobody ever wants to hear—"It's cancer"—a fragment of a Scripture passage came to me: "He knows the way that I take." As I lay there watching the darkness gather around me, I had an instant word from God that said, "I know, Kay, the way you're getting ready to take. The darkness is not dark to me. I will be with you on this unexpected journey."

That night I looked in my Bible and found that the verse came from Job 23:10, as Job affirmed his faith in God in the midst of suffering. I had heard and read that verse enough in my life that it was in my mind when I needed it.

I wish I could tell you that God's Word is the joy of my heart on a daily basis. Some days it isn't. Some days I forget that it is his Word that brings me joy and that his Word is truthful. Jeremiah tells God, "When your words came, I ate them; they were my joy and my heart's delight" (Jer. 15:16). I long for this to be true every day in my life! God's words are so valuable and so precious that when we meditate on them, they will fill our hearts with delight.

Psalm 19:8 says, "The precepts of the LORD are right, giving joy to the heart. The commands of the LORD are radiant, giving light to the eyes." Another translation of that same verse says, "The life-maps of GOD are right, showing the way to joy" (Message). Psalm 119:111 says, "Your commandments are my eternal possession; they are the joy of my heart" (GNT).

Maybe you're new to reading the Bible and some of it doesn't make sense to you yet. That's okay. It takes time to think about and contemplate how the Bible applies to your life. Becoming comfortable with being a Christ follower and becoming comfortable with God's Word are sort of like learning about a culture different from the one you were raised in. At first, the language seems difficult to understand, the cultural customs seem a bit odd, and you're never quite sure if you're doing the right thing at the right moment! But eventually, it starts to make sense to you. And then it not only makes sense but also brings you great joy.

One beautiful way to begin to value and be transformed by God's Word is to read Psalm 119 and meditate on the benefits for those who read Scripture, who know it, who memorize it. It's the truth that we base our lives on, and putting it in our minds is a powerful way to know God more deeply.

God's Works Are Awe-Inspiring

Consider two of the many verses in the Bible that connect joy with God's creation:

> God's works are so great. Worth a lifetime of study—endless enjoyment. (Ps. 111:2 Message)

> The grasslands of the desert overflow;
> the hills are clothed with gladness.
> The meadows are covered with flocks
> and the valleys are mantled with grain;
> they shout for joy and sing.
> Psalm 65:12–13

Not all of us live near gorgeous mountains or rolling ocean waves. But we can stare at a tree in the breeze for a while. We can spend a few minutes studying the intricacies of a blackberry. We can watch an ant on the driveway carry a huge piece of grass back home.

In 1 Chronicles, we read, "Let the trees of the forest sing, let them sing for joy before the LORD" (16:33). This poetic verse claims that God's works actually sing to him! I can't hear the music, but apparently God can. (I've often wondered if they sing on a frequency designed only for his ears, in much the same way only dogs can hear the high-pitched whine of a whistle that causes them to cover their ears.) This is not equivalent to a New Age assertion that there is life or "spirit" in everything—every rock, every bug, every twig on the ground, and every person—but Scripture makes it clear that somehow God's works "sing" praises to him. Sometimes on a windy day my imagination gets away from me. In my mind's eye, the aspen trees are engaged in an exquisitely choreographed performance of song and dance for their Creator. I strain to catch the melody sung by the rippling leaves, but it's no use; my ears can't hear it.

Then I wonder, if all of creation sings, why don't I? If the trees, the flowers, the oceans, the mountains, the clouds, and the animals are praising God's name every day, why don't I—the crown of his creation—sing praise to him? Do I hold back my songs of praise for trivialities as small as no parking space at the crowded mall? My hair didn't curl the way I wanted it to? It's raining? The price of gasoline went up again? All of God's works sing for joy before him, and when I meditate on what he has made, on his stunning abilities as the master Creator, I too sing. I too shout for joy!

I didn't grow up in a denomination that shouted praises to God; we were a pretty reserved crowd. But in the past few years, I've made a startling discovery: Sometimes only shouting my praise will do. And it's not during the times you might anticipate. I rarely feel the need to shout my praise when I'm happy but rather in my most distressing, desperate moments when I do it almost as an act of defiance against Satan, the enemy of joy. He plots how best to steal joy out of my soul, and at my lowest, he almost succeeds. With a rasp in my throat, I let loose with thunderous affirmations of praise to God, echoing Psalm 98:4: "Shout for joy to the LORD, all the earth, burst into jubilant song with music." With my face upturned, sometimes with tears coursing down my face, I declare to the whole universe that nothing—*nothing*—can keep me from worshiping my faithful God.

So today, will you sing? Will you study what God has made and be amazed at his works and praise him? You can choose to do so, no matter what kind of a day you're having, no matter what your feelings tell you, no matter what mood you're in. You can make a choice to rejoice today. Philippians 4:4 says, "Celebrate God all day, every day. I mean, revel in him!" (Message). Psalm 92:4 says, "You make me glad by your deeds, O LORD; I sing for joy at the works of your hands." *Here I am, God, to tell you that you are worthy, that you are reliable, that I trust you, and that I am lifting my voice in praise to you.*

You don't have to have a great voice to sing praises. You can croak like a toad or bark like a dog. A joyful noise is sufficient. What God cares about is your heart's ability to enter into praise for who he is and what he has made. And every once in a while, go ahead and do some shouting; it will do your soul good.

God's Ways Are Loving

As we meditate—ponder, reflect, consider, review, and ruminate—on God's worth, his Word, and his works, we will begin to see a shift in our perspective about our circumstances. Choosing to meditate on his loving ways will carry us through some of life's rough spots.

Psalm 18:35 says, "You protect me with salvation-armor; you hold me up with a firm hand, caress me with your gentle ways" (Message). I would be lying if I told you that I've never questioned God's love for me. There have been some terrible moments when I did not perceive God's hand on my life to be a gentle touch. Sometimes I have felt his hand on my life as a heavy weight that I found hard to bear. Maybe you know exactly what I'm talking about because you, too, have wondered how a loving God could allow *this* to happen.

Those are the moments when Satan jumps in with his suggestions to doubt God, to stop believing that God is good or loving, to give up on our faith. We must deliberately choose to remind ourselves who God is: God has been faithful before; he'll be faithful again. As Carol Kent says, "We realized that when unthinkable circumstances enter your life there comes a point when you either stand by what you believe or you walk away from it."[2] Those are the moments when knowing and believing God's Word are critical, because they draw us back to verses like this: "His love has taken over our lives; God's faithful ways are eternal" (Ps. 117:2 Message) and, "The Lord is faithful to all his promises and loving toward all he has made" (Ps. 145:13).

God's Word is the lifeline that helps me remember God's kindness in the past. I remember times when I didn't think he was loving but later was able to recognize how he had redeemed the pain and made something beautiful from the devastation.

I am a huge fan of stained glass and mosaics—not the ones you make from a kit purchased through a craft catalog—but the ones in which an artist takes multicolored shards of shattered glass or tile and forms a masterpiece worthy of display in a majestic cathedral. The spiritual implications are so obvious. These splendid creations awaken my soul to surrender the splintered pieces of who I am to God's loving touch, to await his artful rearrangement of them into something of beauty. The waiting period may last years longer than I would choose, and it's entirely possible I won't know the full beauty of my pieced-together life until eternity, but make no mistake: God's ways are loving.

When we question the love of God, where does joy fit in? Nowhere! It evaporates. It's gone. Meditating on his loving ways—whether or not we understand them, feel them, or experience them the way we anticipate—keeps joy alive and well.

God's Will Is Good

I'm a white-knuckle flyer; I really don't care for it at all. The only reason I don't travel just by car, train, and boat is that I promised God I would not let fear stop me from doing something I felt was his will. His will has clearly led me to be a *global* advocate for people with HIV and AIDS and for orphans and vulnerable children, so flying is a necessity.

The thing I hate most about flying—besides sitting on the runway in a snowstorm while the plane is being deiced—is when the plane suddenly encounters a storm. Normally, I choose a window seat and leave the plastic shade open the whole time. But in a storm, I have found that if I close the shade, my fear level is more manageable; if all I can see out the window is a gray mist, it terrifies me. I have the sensation that I'm no longer in control. Of course, I never had control to begin with, but I had the illusion of control! I start to think, *If I can't see, the pilot can't see, and if he can't see, we're going down!*

Many times in our lives we feel as if we're flying blind. Circumstances have left us confused, baffled, and unsure; all seems shrouded in mist. We start to panic and cry out to God, *It's dark out there. I can't even see! And God, if I can't see, then maybe you can't see. And if you can't see, I'm going down for sure!*

Just as I have to mentally interrupt the physical panic I encounter when storms or turbulence shake the plane, I have to interrupt the spiritual panic that begins to multiply when a situation feels out of control. Meditating on who God is reminds us that his will is good. He *does* see the darkness around us, but he sees beyond it as well. Jeremiah 29:11 says, "'I know the plans I have for you,' declares the LORD, 'plans to prosper you and not to harm you, plans to give you hope and a future.'"

Because God's will is good, we can embrace joy rather than fear. When we truly believe God's will is good, we have no reason to fear.

The Value System of Heaven

At this point, you may wonder, How does meditating on who God is—his worth, Word, works, ways, and will—give me joy? How does it create the transformation you're talking about?

We've been talking about the way we think—how we develop unwavering convictions about God—so that we approach our problems with a joyful mind-set. The pathway requires us to move from a negative, rebellious, fearful outlook that says, *God, I don't trust you, I don't understand what you're doing, and until you explain it to me and make the hard stuff stop, I won't worship you*, to a more positive, hopeful outlook that says, *God, I trust you no matter what. God, I will be yours until the day you come for me. I will not walk away from you. I believe that your worth is incomparable. I believe that your Word is reliable. I believe that your works are beautiful. I believe that your ways are loving. I believe that your will is good. I believe all these things about you, despite what I see.*

Because God's will is good, we can embrace joy rather than fear.

As you change the way you think about God and who he is, your value system begins to shift and you adopt the "value system of heaven." Many years ago, I had the privilege of learning from Russell Kelfer, a simple country man who taught Sunday school in San Antonio, Texas. He never achieved worldly fame or acclaim, but I'm pretty sure that when I get to heaven, Russell will have a place of prominence. Just a regular guy, he had wisdom and insight into spiritual things unlike anyone I've ever met, and it was he who opened my eyes to the value system of heaven.

What does God value? God values character over comfort, faith over fear, mercy over judgment, justice over injustice, people over possessions, truth over falsehood, humility over pride, hope over despair, love over apathy. In other words, God values the things that will last. He has an eternal perspective. He invites us to view life from that same perspective, to believe that he is at work in history in ways that often remain mysterious to us, that he is redeeming what has been stolen and healing what has been broken.

The apostle Paul is a favorite of mine because of the way he lived out his faith. Like Jesus, Paul was well acquainted with suffering. He explains it in great detail in 2 Corinthians 11:23–28. His suffering included beatings, shipwrecks, starvation, and loneliness. In fact, he composed the book of Philippians while imprisoned for preaching the gospel. Even when he was in chains on the outside, on the inside he was free. Through it all—or perhaps even *because* of it all—Paul was joyful enough to write, "Rejoice in the Lord always"; "In everything give thanks"; "I can do all things through Christ who strengthens me"; "Whether I have little or have much I'm content"; and "We rejoice in our suffering."

Paul wasn't a brainwashed, robotic machine who was oblivious to the pain of the blows, the gnawing hunger of starvation, or the misery of a night in the freezing sea. He didn't sit in a cold, dank prison cell chained to a Roman guard saying, "I like this!"

No. He was a human being. If you had asked him whether he would choose a life that was comfortable or uncomfortable, he probably would have said, "Who wouldn't want to be comfortable? I'd rather not be sitting on this cold, hard prison floor. I'd rather not have my arm chained to another human being all the time. I'd rather have a couple of warm blankets. I'd rather have my friends around me. I'd rather be traveling around the Roman Empire talking about Jesus. But if this is where God asks me to be, this is where I'll be. And I will choose joy in this place."

Paul had learned long before that God was the only true source of joy for him. He had already experienced the pain of friends who abandoned him, cities that closed their doors to him, earthly possessions that couldn't satisfy, an education that couldn't save him, and a personality that often got him into trouble. No, God was Paul's only true source of joy, and because of that, he consistently, faithfully chose to focus not on what he could see with his eyes but on what he could see with his spirit.

No wonder Paul can urge us two thousand years later to rejoice, to give thanks in everything, to be content with what we have, to be patient in affliction, and to not lose heart. Heaven's value system was his, and so were heaven's joys.

Paul did something I want to do every day. I want to see my losses, my disappointments, my heartaches, my pain, and my sorrow through God's value system. That's why Paul had joy: He chose the value system of heaven over and over again.

He wrote this passionate affirmation of faith in 2 Corinthians 4:16–18: "We do not lose heart. Though outwardly we are wasting away, yet inwardly we are being renewed day by day. For our light and momentary troubles are achieving for us an eternal glory that far outweighs them all. So we fix our eyes not on what is seen, but on what is unseen. For what is seen is temporary, but what is unseen is eternal."

If there is a secret to joy, this is it: Choose the eternal over the temporary.

When you and I choose the temporary over the eternal, putting our fragile hopes for joy in even more fragile earthly sources, we will be disappointed. But when we put our fragile hopes in God, we become confident and assured—not of an outcome but of a Person. *He is our only true source of joy!*

—— **PRAYER** ——

Lord, teach me how to align my value system with yours. Help me to choose the eternal over the temporary. I'm not good at this. I flub it more than I get it right. God, build in me a settled assurance that you are in control, a confidence that allows me to move into life not destroyed by what happens but believing that ultimately everything will be all right because you are God. From that place I can praise you because your worth, your Word, your works, your ways, and your will do not change. In the name of Jesus Christ, the man of sorrows and yet the man of joy, amen.

FOR REFLECTION AND APPLICATION

1. Take a minute to be still and quiet—ask God to help you be open to what he wants to show you. Prayerfully read Psalm 119. Are there actions you need to take as you seek joy?

2. "God values character over comfort, faith over fear, mercy over judgment, justice over injustice, people over possessions, truth over falsehood, humility over pride, hope over despair, love over apathy." Reflect on your own actions this week. Where did you see the value system of heaven in your life?

— SIX —

Believing Even in Darkness

Through the heartfelt mercies of our God, God's Sunrise will break in upon us, shining on those in the darkness, those sitting in the shadow of death, then showing us the way, one foot at a time, down the path of peace.

Luke 1:78–79 Message

If joy does not arise out of the midst of tragedy, it will not arise at all. Christian joy is rooted in darkness, chaos, meaninglessness, sorrow. . . . Separate joy from sorrow and there's nothing left.

Mike Mason

October 11, 2008, was a Saturday. On my list of things to do that day was to stop by and visit my precious, seven-week-old grandson, Cole. Cole was born five weeks premature, and due to the emergency circumstances surrounding his birth, he almost didn't make it. My heart was still feeling the residue of the emotions that came with nearly losing him on the day he was born, and I just couldn't get enough of holding him, drinking in his baby smell, and nuzzling his fuzzy little head. I also had a secret reason for dropping by the home of my son, Josh, and daughter-in-love, Jaime: I had a strong suspicion that Jaime had a brain tumor.

For weeks following Cole's birth, Jaime just had not been herself, and every day that week she seemed to have a frightening new symptom of something bad: Her head felt heavy, she had headaches, she had double vision, she threw up without nausea.

That Saturday as we talked and visited, she laughingly said, "I can't walk a straight line," and got up and demonstrated. When graceful, athletic Jaime couldn't keep her balance, I KNEW. She and Josh were taking a cautious approach to her physical symptoms, not wanting to rush into a round of fruitless medical tests; they, too, were still reeling from the shock and trauma of Cole's birth. They promised they would see a doctor on Monday if she wasn't feeling any better, but I left their house sick with fear. People have since asked me why I was so positive that Jaime had a brain tumor. Did I have medical training? All I can say is that being a hypochondriac paid off for once!

Several hours later, my son let me know he was taking Jaime to the ER, but it was more of a precaution than a fear that something was really wrong. But soon, a very kind ER physician had the terrible task of informing us that Jaime had a brain tumor and needed to be admitted to the hospital immediately. The tumor was pushing on her optic nerve, which could cause blindness, and even more serious, she had excessive fluid in her brain that was potentially life-threatening.

Everything went into fast motion from that moment. Decisions as to what further tests were needed, where to go for delicate surgery, how to care for our sweet baby Cole consumed us. Within thirty-six hours, she was in UCLA Ronald Reagan Medical Center being prepped for delicate brain surgery to try to remove a tennis-ball-sized tumor. The surgeon speculated that it was a slow-growing benign tumor she had had her entire life, but it was intricately intertwined with vital parts of her brain and extremely vascular, meaning the surgery would be complex, lengthy, and potentially catastrophic.

The day of the surgery seemed like it stretched on and on with no end in sight. The initial surgery took more than twenty agonizing, terrifying hours—with only periodic reports from the operating room. Then Dr. Neil Martin, her very tired surgeon, came into the crowded room where family and friends spilled out into the hallway to let us know the tumor—all except a thumbnail-sized piece on the cerebellum—had been removed. We shouted our relief, our praise, and our joy that she had survived and appeared to be in good shape.

Within the hour, Dr. Martin was back, telling us that Jaime had developed a critical brain bleed and that emergency surgery was required. Barely able to form words, I asked him how long it took before critical turned into fatal; his answer was short and to the point: "It all depends on how quickly we can find the bleed and how quickly we can stop it." And with those heart-stopping words, he ran to the OR.

Another five hours of waiting . . . waiting . . . waiting . . . and hoping and praying. Then finally the good news came that they had found the bleed and had been able to repair it quickly. Now the really scary question: What impairment would Jaime suffer as a result? Too soon to tell, we were informed.

Within two weeks, Jaime needed one more surgery. The cerebrospinal fluid was not draining properly, and she needed an internal cranial shunt. With a 60 percent chance of success, she went back into the OR. It worked!

During the next month, we watched, dumbfounded with delight, as day by day Jaime beat all the odds. She came off the ventilator in days, was able to eat although her throat was partially paralyzed, slowly regained her vision, began to smile, and then the big victory—she walked. We thought in our hearts that she was a miracle, but when one of the doctors observed her take her first walk down the hospital halls holding on to a walker and a nurse, he had tears in his eyes. "A miracle," he muttered under his breath. Today, the left side of her head carries the impact of the tumor and the surgeries: no hearing in her left ear, no tears, no nasal discharge, and no taste buds on that side—but in the overall scheme of things, very small impairments. She is still Jaime—no physical or emotional impairments, no personality changes, no mental losses.

In the span of three months, my family rode an emotional roller coaster: Cole came into the world early and nearly died, Jaime had three brain surgeries and nearly died, and a loved one was hospitalized for mental illness. Even as we rejoiced that Jaime was alive and thriving, that Cole had survived his perilous birth experience, and that the loved one was making progress, the three months of nonstop fear, near loss, trauma, drama, pain, and suffering took its toll on our family. Our incredible support system of friends and family rallied around us in ways we will never forget, but still I lost about one-third of my hair from the stress, ended up with a knee injury (from too much standing on a hard floor) that required surgery, and had nightmares in which I relived each scary moment.

Opening the Door to Joy

Birth and near death, illness and recovery, tragedies and miracles, joy and sorrow. A perfect picture of life as we know it. The parallel train tracks of joy and sorrow are always running side by side throughout our lives. Choosing to believe in the darkness—in our personal lives and on a global scale—opens the door to joy.

Some of you might be overwhelmed by the sufferings of my family compared to yours, but others of you could top my stories in a heartbeat; the pile of suffering you have or are enduring gets higher with each passing day. The point is not about who suffers the most, or how someone else handles the suffering, but how you handle the suffering that comes your way.

I used to think that when intense suffering came my way, it was an enemy meant to destroy me. While it is true that some of Satan's favorite weapons against Christ followers are illness, pain, and loss, I'm also learning that God uses intense suffering to reveal to us great wealth that is hidden in the secret places of sorrow. A Bible story tucked in the book of Isaiah illustrates this truth beautifully.

Isaiah tells the story of the nation of Israel's rebellion against God, resulting in the entire nation being taken captive by the Babylonians. For thirty-nine chapters, the prophet Isaiah details Israel's many sins and failures and the reasons for God's punishment.

But in Isaiah 40 and following, he begins to encourage them that God has not forgotten about them or discarded them, even though they failed to honor him as their God. Not only will God eventually put all things right in the world through the coming of the Messiah, Jesus, but he will also redeem Israel from captivity through a Gentile king, Cyrus. God promises that Cyrus will find hidden treasures of jewels and gold that will bring him unbelievable wealth. This fortune will help him fulfill the destiny God has in store for him by funding his military conquests.

Now, I love to know that we serve a God who fulfills his promises. He said that Cyrus would become king, that he would become fabulously wealthy, and that he would be used by God to free Israel, and it happened exactly the way God promised. To see God fulfill his pledge of release and rescue to Israel strengthens my faith.

But I have to tell you that recently, late one night, I was desperately seeking comfort for intense suffering in my life, and I didn't care much about Cyrus or Babylon or Israel. I was feeling anguish for a loved one who has lived with a biochemical disorder for a very long time. I was anxiously looking ahead to a situation that I thought might end very poorly, in a way that would break my heart even more. I thought, *I can't bear this suffering, God. I can't bear this darkness that surrounds me and my loved one. I need you tonight.* Even though we had gone through much darkness with Cole's birth, Jaime's illness, and the psychiatric hospitalization, I had not yet learned all that God wanted to teach me about how to experience joy in the depths of suffering.

So I opened a Bible computer program and began to hunt from Genesis to Revelation for every verse I could find that

mentioned "dark" and "darkness" and quickly compiled
about twenty pages of references. I found verses that com-
forted me and some that confused me, but most of all I
realized I wasn't the first person to cry out to God in the
darkness of my circumstances.

In 2 Samuel 22:12, King David says that God has wrapped
himself in a "trenchcoat of black rain-cloud darkness" (Message). *Yes! That's exactly what I feel like, God! I feel like you're
hiding from me and I can't find you!* I identified with Job in
Job 19:8: "He has blocked my way so I cannot pass; he has
shrouded my paths in darkness." *God, I can't get past the bar-
ricades you've erected; I'm in total darkness.* My soul echoed
King David's desperate plea in Psalm 13:3: "Answer me, O
Lord my God; give me light in my darkness lest I die" (TLB).

By this time—having scanned verses all the way to Isaiah—I found myself heartily agreeing with the biblical characters when they angrily accused God and chastised him
for his seeming absence in their troubles. When I got to the
story of Cyrus in Isaiah 45, the prophetic words jumped off
the page. The power of God's promise stunned me so much
that I actually gasped out loud:

> I will give you the treasures of darkness,
>> riches stored in secret places,
> so that you may know that I am the LORD,
>> the God of Israel, who summons you by name.
>>>> Isaiah 45:3

My first thought was, *I don't want to be in this darkness.
I don't want my loved one to be in darkness. I want out of
this dark place NOW.*

My second thought was, Can this really be true? Can there
be treasures hidden in this darkness?

My next thought was, If there are treasures in this darkness, I don't think I want them. Thanks anyway. Because it probably means I will only find them if I'm in this pain, and God, I don't want to be in this pain anymore.

All I could see in that moment was the track of sorrow in my life; joy was nowhere near. The immediate challenge was to believe that treasures in the darkness actually exist and then to believe I could find them. And yes, I had to accept and embrace the truth that these treasures are a special category of gifts from God, hidden riches ONLY to be found in the secret places of my deepest pain and agony.

One of my favorite authors, Henri Nouwen, says, "Our cup is often so full of pain that joy seems completely unreachable. When we are crushed like grapes, we cannot think of the wine we will become."[1]

I had to make a decision, and you do too: Will I surrender to God in the darkness, believing that I will find treasures of joy, blessing, and meaning here? Although I didn't like it, God had allowed me to be in that dark place. I had to decide whether I would embrace it so he could lead me to the treasures I could only find in suffering.

Maybe as you're reading this you're thinking, I haven't known that kind of darkness. Growing up, my family life wasn't perfect, but it was warm and nurturing, or at least pleasant. I did pretty well in school, had moderate success in athletics or academics, and was moderately popular. I've had no major health scares so far. I'm not wealthy, but I always seem to have enough to get by. Things are going pretty well for me right now. A lot of what she's saying doesn't really apply to me.

If that's what you're thinking, it might be wise to go ahead and start preparing to seek treasures of joy in the darkness

NOW. Because the darkness will come. I'm not saying that to scare you. But the reality is, this is earth, not heaven. Sin, pain, illness, loss, separation, grief, mental illness, financial ruin, death, and a whole host of other terrible circumstances happen on a daily basis, and each of us needs to be prepared for dark days. And the thing is, you don't prepare for the emotional darkness by stockpiling canned food or reading survival manuals or staying up at night dreading the future and being paralyzed by it. What I'm suggesting you do is what the apostle Paul instructed us in Colossians 2:7:

> Let your roots grow down into him, and let your lives be built on him. Then your faith will grow strong in the truth you were taught, and you will overflow with thankfulness. (NLT)

I encourage you to deliberately send your roots down deep in Jesus today so that your faith becomes rich, intimate, and stable, enabling you to withstand the worst this world can throw at you. I want you to be able to find the treasures of joy when the darkness is so thick you can't even see your hand in front of your face.

We learn that Cyrus found riches hidden in darkness, just as the prophecy had said in Isaiah 45:3. But I don't believe that verse is just about Cyrus. God is telling us that just as he enriched a Gentile king so he could fulfill his mission, God will enrich you and me with riches in secret places that will enable us to fulfill his call on our lives.

So as we talk about joy—true treasure—hidden in suffering, my first challenge to you is to decide if you'll believe that God has a plan. Will you believe that he has promised you treasure and you can seek it? Will you believe that even in the darkness you are experiencing God can give you joy?

From Trash to Treasure

Do you remember doing scavenger hunts as a kid? It's a great, low-tech game that I played many times growing up. In case you've never experienced the thrill of a scavenger hunt, let me explain it to you. The point of the game is for you and your friends to make a list of weird, random items that your neighbors might have—bubble-gum–flavored dental floss, a wooden clothespin, a red plastic Checkers piece—and then run feverishly from house to house ahead of your friends to see if your neighbors will part with their "treasures." Whoever collects the most items on the list wins the game. It was so much fun to bring back those little pieces of flotsam and jetsam—you never knew your neighbors were so strange until you knocked on their door and found they actually had a pair of Christmas socks with light-up toes that you could borrow!

But the things you collect on a scavenger hunt are, let's admit it, basically trash. Nobody really thinks the bits of odds and ends are treasures.

We sometimes think that God plays a cruel game with us; he wants us to go on a spiritual scavenger hunt for "treasures" that are really trash. But God makes it clear that he wants to give us real treasure, real joy, real contentment. Something incredibly valuable. Something that will make us spiritually rich; definitely not trash disguised as treasure.

The Bible says in 1 Peter 1:7, "These trials will show that your faith is genuine. It is being tested as fire tests and purifies gold—though your faith is far more precious than mere gold. So when your faith remains strong through many trials, it will bring you much praise and glory and honor on the day when Jesus Christ is revealed to the whole world" (NLT).

For me, the process of turning trash into treasure is ongoing and will continue until God takes me to heaven. But in the meantime, let me share with you how some of that ugly trash has turned into treasure.

As I told you, in 2003, I was diagnosed with stage-one breast cancer. A year and a half later, I was diagnosed with stage-one melanoma. Through the fiery trial of cancer, God produced gold in my life, something that has lasted and something that brings joy. One trash-to-treasure gift God gave me is a new ability to relate to people who have a life-threatening illness. I was already an advocate for people with HIV and AIDS before my cancer diagnosis, but after I'd experienced cancer, I could look into the eyes of people around the world and say to them, "I don't know what it's like to be HIV positive, but I do know what it's like to be given a life-threatening diagnosis." I experienced new levels of empathy and compassion I never could have attained without going through cancer.

God makes it clear that he wants to give us real treasure, real joy, real contentment.

I've also learned that I can stare death in the face. I used to be very, very afraid to die. It wasn't that I was afraid of what would happen to me after death because I was certain of my salvation through Jesus Christ, but I was afraid of the process of dying. God has shown me that I don't need to be afraid. That "treasure"—freedom from fear—has brought great joy in my life.

I've gained an appreciation for how precious and fragile life is. I don't assume anymore that I'm going to grow old and sit on the porch in a rocking chair with my husband and watch the sun set. I understand now that in a brief moment life can change forever. But realizing that brings me joy in the current moment, not fear for the future. Every day when I get up, I live more passionately and purposely than I ever did before because I don't know about tomorrow—God still owns tomorrow—all I know about is today.

I gained a more intimate walk with Jesus as I had to trust him in ways I had never trusted him before. I had to trust him with the fact that I might leave my husband and children and not see my grandchildren grow up. I had to trust him with the fact that my diagnosis came just six months after I began to visit Africa. I found myself praying, *You called me to be an advocate, and now I might die?* I learned to trust God in those places.

I have also grown in my appreciation for and anticipation of heaven. Heaven looks so much more beautiful to me because I know that in heaven broken bodies and broken minds are finally healed and restored.

What a joy to be able to relate to others who suffer, to say that I know what it's like. What a joy to live knowing that life is brief and every day counts. What a joy to look at my family and my friends and tell them that they matter and I want to spend time with them. What a joy to live every day knowing that heaven is a place of healing! This is a joy that comes not in spite of suffering but because of suffering. I am in awe of the treasures, the hidden riches of joy, I have found in the secret places of the darkness.

--- **PRAYER** ---

Father, help me to see treasures of joy in the darkness of my life. I want to believe you have gold hidden in secret places when I go through hard times. Forgive me for believing the lie that suffering is nothing but an enemy to harm me instead of believing that you are my friend. You are there to walk with me and show me treasures I wouldn't have seen any other way. Keep me from rejecting the gift of joy that sorrow brings. May I seek you as the one who is close, who is intimate, who calls me by name. May the pain I am in push me toward a great passion for you and a greater joy in you. In the name of Jesus, amen.

FOR REFLECTION AND APPLICATION

1. Think about a time of deep sorrow in your life, one that has passed. What treasure did you find?

2. If a loved one described you to someone, what would you like to hear them say? What would it take for them to describe you as a person of joy?

PART 3

JOY Is A CONDITION OF MY HEART

Cultivating a Soul-Response
That Allows Joy to Deepen

Once again, my overly sensitive spirit had been crushed by conflict—this time with a much-loved friend. My automatic self-protective defenses were armed and ready to go, but I couldn't decide if I wanted to let loose with hurtful words or just retreat to the cozy darkness of self-pity and depression.

Another option presented itself as I remembered Jeremiah 2:13 and the powerful visual of digging my own cisterns to find joy. Here was a perfect opportunity to deliberately, intentionally, and purposefully place my joy not in a friend, who represented a cistern that couldn't hold water, but in the God who will never leave me or abandon me—even when I've fallen short of my best behavior. *You are my source of joy, God; I choose you*, I whispered to myself.

The conflict still had to be resolved, but I came at it from a place of spiritual renewal and strength, no longer unrealistically seeking joy from a frail human being like myself but confident that I had a Friend whose presence in my life was permanent.

You might not be ready to say boldly, "God, you are the only source of joy for me." Maybe you can only halfheartedly whisper those words on certain days. Perhaps you are at the stage where you can only cautiously think it. But even if you just allow the thought in your mind, that's progress! That's the beginning of where God wants to take you. Over time, as you and I put our hope and trust in God and meditate on who he is, we will start to take on the value system of heaven. And joy grows in the value system of heaven because it's based not on external circumstances but on inward certainty.

Like a carefully tended crop, joy grows when we take the time to plant, water, weed, and wait for the harvest. Mike Mason says, "The direction of joy isn't always up. Often to be joyful we must go down—down through the noise of racing thoughts, down through the swirling chaos of circumstances, down through the deceptive appearances of life, down into the still waters and green pastures at the heart's core."[1]

But make no mistake: Joy can grow in you! Do you want it? What are you willing to do to help it take root in your soul? Remember, we have an enemy who loves nothing more than to see us in a sobbing heap on the floor—shattered, discouraged, and hopeless. If you want it, you're going to have to fight for it. If you think that experiencing joy comes naturally, you haven't been listening. Happiness requires no effort on our part, but joy results from our deliberate choices to think differently, act differently, and feel differently. Happiness comes unbidden and unexpectedly and can leave just as abruptly; joy can be available anytime, anywhere, any place—but it is a result of our decision to choose it.

There are specific actions you can take that will allow the delicate seedling of joy to mature into a robust, sturdy plant that can withstand hurricane-velocity winds, but you must choose to tenderly nurture it deep within you. In this section, we're going to look at those actions that lead to quiet confidence in our emotions and attitudes so that when bad things happen, we already have the soul-response we need to respond with joy. Not only can we grow in our ability to nurture joy in ourselves, but we can also become skilled at nurturing it in others.

SEVEN

Nurturing Joy in Yourself

To all who mourn in Israel,
  he will give a crown of beauty for ashes;
a joyous blessing instead of mourning,
  festive praise instead of despair.

Isaiah 61:3 NLT

The walls we build around us to keep sadness out also keep out the joy.

Jim Rohn

As I sought to discover how to live a joyful life, I made a surprising discovery about myself. As much as I say I want to become more joyful, I often actively sabotage it in myself and others. Instead of cultivating heart-responses that allow me to shine like a star on a dark night, I have found myself working overtime at beating

117

down the hints of joy that start to blossom. Sometimes it's because of the huge, overwhelming circumstances of life that come as uninvited guests and I feel powerless to change, but other times joy evaporates because of decisions and choices I make in matters of relative unimportance. I don't want to do that anymore. Instead of being a joy killer, I want to be a joy builder. I'm ready to learn the tools that will allow joy to take root. Let's look at four ways to nurture and build joy in our souls.

Focus on Grace

By the time I went to college, I had a sincere heart but a serious misunderstanding of how to please God. I had grown up convinced that if I just did the right things, God would love me; keeping the rules was my ticket to becoming a great woman of faith. *Grace* was a woman's name, not something connected with God.

Rick and I came of age during the turbulence of the late 60s and mid-70s—you know, hippies, Vietnam, the civil rights movement, the sexual revolution, Woodstock, and best of all, the Jesus Movement.

The Jesus Movement, with its emphasis on passionate worship and radical discipleship, exploded on the national scene through music, art, and fiery preaching. Suddenly, racially segregated churches with robed choirs sedately singing hymns and pastors preaching the same old messages in the same old way weren't cool. Being *nice* and fitting in with the status quo of their parents' world ceased to be the goal of young adults. Long-haired young men and women took the radical Jesus of the Bible seriously, and their passionate messages of disciplined obedience, death to self-interest, and sacrificial love shook the country.

As the Jesus Movement swept through our small Christian college, I was ripe for something beyond the safe Christianity I had grown up with. I was captivated by the desire to *be something* for God. Unfortunately, I brought my misunderstanding about God's grace into the mix, and instant obedience—rule-following—became a god in and of itself.

One of the first "rules" I began to follow was no wearing of makeup. As a natural blond, I have almost no eyelashes and eyebrows, so this decision had serious implications for my appearance! Looking back at old photographs, I see a pale, washed-out girl, but I felt I was godly and pleasing to God. Next, I decided that wearing fingernail polish was also carnal and a waste of money, so I quit painting my nails. Then came the firm decision never to wear a swimsuit in public again. No more shorts. No more jewelry. And, to prove the depth of my spirituality, I got up at four a.m. to pray. Everybody knows that women who get up at four a.m. to pray are much more spiritual than those who get up at seven, right?

But here's the sad part. Instead of producing joy in my life, these self-inflicted rules produced a potent case of self-righteousness. I'd see another girl on my Christian college campus and think, *Look at that girl with shorts on. I'll bet she's a seven a.m. pray-er! Lightweight!*

My rule-keeping also produced a fear that I could never do enough to please God. After all, every group I hung out with had a different set of rules. How would I figure out all the *right* rules? I thought that if I could just do the right things in the right way, God would love me more. By focusing on the rules, I completely missed the relationship.

Maybe for you a rule is nothing more than something to be broken, and moving beyond rigid rule-following sounds like a piece of cake. I don't understand that point of view—it remains challenging for me at times because I'm still a dyed-in-the-wool rule follower! I like rules—they keep me safe and make life manageable. Well, I should clarify. I like the rules *I* make, not someone else's rules. *My* rules make sense. Yours might not. What a hypocrite I can be! But God gives us the entire book of Galatians to teach us that rules by themselves cannot give us joy.

Galatians 3:12 tells us that rule-keeping was never meant to be the way to a relationship with God: "Rule-keeping does not naturally evolve into living by faith, but only perpetuates itself in more and more rule-keeping" (Message). Verse 22 says, "If any kind of rule-keeping had power to create life in us, we would certainly have gotten it by this time" (Message). Could it get any clearer? Rules don't produce life. They don't produce joy. Relationship does.

Ephesians 1:4–7 tells us how that relationship with God occurs. "Even before he made the world, God loved us and chose us in Christ to be holy and without fault in his eyes. God decided in advance to adopt us into his own family by bringing us to himself through Jesus Christ. This is what he wanted to do, and it gave him great pleasure" (NLT).

When I became a Christian, God placed me "in Christ," and I am now completely acceptable to him. This concept is so important that the phrase "in Christ" is used twelve times in Ephesians 1. God wants to make the point that rule-keeping isn't the key to relationship; being "in Christ" is.

The fact that God accepts me was difficult for me to understand until I saw an illustration that really stuck with me. I'd like for you to pause in your reading and take two minutes to do this exercise so that you get the full impact of the sweet truth about God's acceptance of you.

Find a small piece of paper—any paper will do. Crumple it up and then unfold it. Smudge it with ink or dirt. Rip the edges in several places. You should have a really messy piece of paper in your hands!

This paper represents your life before you came to Jesus Christ—pretty messy and not worth much. The rips and the tears and the smudges represent the mistakes you made. I'll bet that you hope (like I do) that some of those mistakes are known only to God. We're all ashamed of some of the choices we've made in life, some of the activities we've participated in and words we've said.

Now take that torn piece of paper and put it inside this book—anywhere—and then close the book tightly. Hold the book in your hands and see if you can tell where that piece of paper is. Turn the book over in your hands in different directions. If it's small enough, you shouldn't be able to see the paper at all. The paper is "in" the book, and if you didn't know any better, you wouldn't have a clue that the book held a small, torn, messy piece of paper.

This, my friends, is what God did for us when we brought our tattered souls to him for salvation: He took us and put us "in" Jesus Christ. We are now "in Christ," and when God looks at us—even if he turns in every possible direction—all he can see is the perfect righteousness of his beloved Son, Jesus. Just as this book physically covered your piece of paper, enveloping it in the clean pages, Jesus has spiritually covered your messy, sinful soul, enveloping you in the pure, clean, spotless "rightness" that is his. You are accepted in Christ.

As C. S. Lewis points out, "Christ died for men precisely because men are not worth dying for; to make them worth it."[1] In Christ, God will never love you any more than he does now, and he will never love you any less. His acceptance is based not on your performance but on Christ's perfection, which never changes.

Because fellow humans who are supposed to love us well don't always do a very good job, we project that inadequate human love onto God. If we could ever begin to truly grasp the depth of the love God has for us, it would forever change the way we view him, the plans he has for us, and the way we see ourselves.

The truth is that human love gets tired and weary and can fade in the dailyness of being together over time. We hesitate to "bother" family and friends with our worries or anxieties, fearful we will wear out our welcome. When those closest to us have carried us in our moments of weakness one too many times, we are tempted to believe we have become a burden to them.

But to God we are never a bother or a burden but his beloved. Such a tender expression of care, rich in meaning, speaks to the deepest longings of our hearts. To be God's beloved means we are cherished, treasured, valued, and yearned for. He doesn't tolerate you; he adores you!

How do we know that's the way he feels about us? His Book of Joy tells us so. God calls Jesus his beloved Son (Matt. 3:17), and Ephesians 1 says I am spiritually *in* Jesus Christ; that means if Jesus is God's beloved, then I am too.

And it brings praise to God because of his wonderful grace. God gave that grace to us freely, in Christ, the One he loves. (Eph. 1:6 NCV)

Many verses confirm we are the beloved of God, but here are just two more:

So, as those who have been chosen of God, holy and beloved.
(Col. 3:12 NASB)

But we should always give thanks to God for you, brethren
beloved by the Lord, because God has chosen you from the
beginning for salvation through sanctification by the Spirit
and faith in the truth. (2 Thess. 2:13 NASB)

If you've ever wondered if God REALLY loves you, this
spiritual truth should lay that doubt to rest. As Ephesians 1
says, we have been adopted into God's very own family. This
is the most significant proof that he is madly in love with
you: It gave him *great pleasure* to include you in his family!
Isn't it amazing to see God's love for you in his Word? His
heart beats with joy at the thought of you!

I now know that God is telling me, "I love you not because
of anything you've done, not because of any worthiness you
have, not because you rigidly kept all the rules, not because
you were the girl who didn't wear shorts in college. I love you
because I have set my love upon you." That's grace. That's
acceptance. Choosing to believe in God's grace and acceptance of me nurtures joy in the softest places in my soul and
prepares me to trust him for my future.

Trust God for the Future

As this tiny seedling of joy begins to grow within us, it will be
exposed to the potentially toxic test of worry. Nothing kills
joy faster than worry. Some of you are fabulous worriers—
you've elevated worry to an art form. When you're not worrying about your finances, your job, your marriage, your
kids, or your health, you worry about nothing specific, just

so you can continue worrying. You could earn money on the side worrying for other people!

Remember our definition of joy: Joy is the settled assurance that God is in control of all the details of my life, the quiet confidence that ultimately everything is going to be all right, and the determined choice to praise God in all things.

Do you see how trust and joy are related? When trust in God grows, joy has the freedom to grow as well. We cannot have joy and worry at the same time.

A wise friend once told me, "When you're worrying, you're not trusting. And when you're trusting, you're not worrying."

God longs for us to gaze at him in trust with a steady, fixed look and only glance briefly at our problems. My pattern has been to gaze at my problems and only glance at God. When something happens in my life that causes me to worry, the temptation is to focus all my energy and attention on the problem. I can't stop thinking about the situation that has me anxious, and it can overshadow every other aspect of my life—my husband, my job, my ministry, my health. I find myself *gazing* at the problem.

We cannot have joy and worry at the same time.

I wish I could say that the energy I invest in gazing at my troubles is productive—that I come up with solutions or strategies—but unfortunately, many times I experience an endless repetition of the same thoughts I had the day before. And even when I talk to God about the problem—which in essence is still gazing at the problem—my focus is still on the problem itself. Yet I'm talking to a Red Sea God who has the ability to solve it or give me strength to face it, if I would turn my attention to him.

A fundamental part of expressing trust in God is learning how to gaze at him and only glance at our problems. When we get that in reverse and gaze at our problems and only glance at God, joy can't take root in our hearts because we are so focused on ourselves. As the Bible says in 1 Peter 5:7, "You can throw the whole weight of your anxieties upon him, for you are his personal concern" (Phillips). Lack of trust chokes joy in our hearts.

Matthew 6:33–34 says, "Steep your life in God-reality, God-initiative, God-provisions. Don't worry about missing out. You'll find all your everyday human concerns will be met. Give your entire attention to what God is doing right now, and don't get worked up about what may or may not happen tomorrow. God will help you deal with whatever hard things come up when the time comes" (Message).

Another version says, "So don't be anxious about tomorrow. God will take care of your tomorrow too. Live one day at a time" (v. 34 TLB).

If there was ever a Bible passage to put on your bathroom mirror, this is it. I need it written on my hand so I can read it over and over! Maybe I'll get a tattoo: "Live one day at a time!"

Sarah Young, author of *Jesus Calling*, meditated on Scripture and then wrote a daily devotional book as though it was from the perspective of Jesus to his children. This is her interpretation of what the Bible says in Deuteronomy 29:29 and Psalm 32:8 about worry:

> I am leading you step by step, through your life. Hold My hand in trusting dependence, letting Me guide you through this day. Your future looks uncertain and feels flimsy—even precarious. That is how it should be. Secret things belong to

the Lord, and future things are secret things. When you try to figure out the future, you are grasping at things that are Mine. This, like all forms of worry, is an act of rebellion: doubting My promises to care for you. Whenever you find yourself worrying about the future, repent and return to Me. I will show you the next step forward, and the one after that. And the one after that. Relax and enjoy the journey in My presence, trusting Me to open up the way before you as you go.[2]

I was shocked when I pondered her assertion that worry—doubting God's promises to care for me—is a form of rebellion. I don't want to live in rebellion toward God in even the slightest way, do you? But it makes sense. God has promised repeatedly to care for us, reassuring us that he knows our needs even before we ask. We're his beloved! When we refuse to believe him—as evidenced by our tension headaches, chewed-up fingernails, irritability, stomachaches, and sleepless nights—we are saying, "I know you were there for me in the past, but what about now? I'm not sure you can be counted on, God, so I had better figure this out on my own." And that is a complete lack of trust, which is a quiet form of rebellion.

Many years ago, Rick and I took our first international trip away from our children, who were very young at the time. As you know, I don't like to fly. Back then, I really hated it. Weeks before we left, I began to contemplate the plane trip that would take me far away from my children for ten days. Every night I had cold sweats as I lay awake envisioning all the terrible scenarios that were going to happen while I wasn't there to control everything.

First of all, I was convinced that Rick and I were going to die in a plane crash. The second thing that was going to happen was my children were going to die or be seriously injured, even though their grandparents were extremely responsible. I worried that our house was going to burn down. To top off my out-of-control fears, I envisioned our church members rallying behind some other pastor and kicking us out of Saddleback Church. I was crazy with anxiety.

I repeatedly said to Rick, "I'm so scared. What if we die, or the kids die, or the house burns, or you lose your job?" He would patiently, but firmly, tell me that everything would be fine. "But you don't know that for sure!" I would tearfully say. "Have you got a crystal ball that tells you we're not going to crash? Has God sent you an email saying that the children will be fine and the house will be fine and your job will be fine?"

My anxiety got so bad that I was going to have to either cancel the trip or do something about it. I finally realized I needed to do some serious business with God.

I turned to the Scriptures. As I was reading, I came upon the story of the angel Gabriel telling Mary, the mother of Jesus, that she was going to bear the Messiah. She must have been absolutely terrified with all the "what ifs" that filled her mind. But what was her response? Immediately—not after weeks of crying and carrying on—she said, "I am the Lord's servant. . . . May it be to me as you have said" (Luke 1:38).

I thought, That's it. God, I don't believe you want me to cancel this trip just because I'm afraid. I trust you. I don't know the future. I can't figure that out. But God, I believe you are enough for me today, and you will be enough for me tomorrow and the tomorrow after that. Let my attitude be the same as Mary's. Let me come to a place of peace.

Inadvertently, I had given my heart away to the lesser gods of fear, anxiety, worry, and depression. Trusting that God was in control of all the details of my life led to a settled, confident peace, but it wasn't the kind of peace you might anticipate. The place of peace I came to was not a reassurance that I wouldn't die. It had nothing to do with my children, my house, or Rick's job. My peace was this: Even if *it's* not okay, *I* will be okay. I will be okay no matter what happens because God is with me and he will be enough. This is the quiet confidence I've been talking about—confidence that God will help you make it through.

That's the kind of peace God is working to create within us day after day. When we come up against the things that frighten us, we are in the best place to develop peace and joy. It is in those places that we have the opportunity to say to God, "I am yours. May it be to me as you have said."

Balance Your Life

Many of us spend our days feeling driven by the almost impossible demands of our lives. More than two thousand years before email, social networking, cell phones, and carpools, the Greek philosopher Socrates said, "Beware the barrenness of the busy life." Joy withers in our lives when we are too busy. Too often we overestimate the amount of time we have to do a task and underestimate the amount of time it's actually going to take to do that task. We end up slaves to commitments we've made, saying yes to all the wrong things, leaving ourselves with no time or energy to say yes to the people closest to us.

When our children or grandchildren ask to play a game, we can't because we have too much to get done. When our spouse needs our attention, we say no because we're just too tired. When a friend needs a listening ear, we're distracted because we have to get back to the office. When we feel a tug to pray about something we heard in church that morning, we forget it on the way to the grocery store. We've given ourselves to pursuits that seem important and left the people closest to us longing for relationship.

I'm convinced most of us are terrific liars when it comes to busyness, but the person we lie to is ourselves. The ability we have to deceive ourselves is epic! When we say, "This is just a busy season," or, "This is only temporary; I won't live like this forever," we fool ourselves into thinking that this frantic pace is just a temporary condition instead of the new normal.

I will be okay no matter what happens because God is with me and he will be enough.

As Annie Dillard says so succinctly, "How we spend our days is, of course, how we spend our lives. What we do with this hour, and that one, is what we are doing."[3] Yes, there are unusual seasons of busyness, but it's far too easy to let a season become a pattern. What becomes a pattern becomes a way of life. And a busy way of life robs us of joy.

In Psalm 127:2, we read, "It is useless to work hard for the food you eat by getting up early and going to bed late. The LORD gives food to those he loves while they sleep" (GW). I don't completely understand this verse because I have yet to wake up in the morning and find that everything got done while I was sleeping! But I know the point is that it is self-defeating to work morning and night, pushing because we think that if something is not done everything will fall apart, and then fall into bed so exhausted that we can't sleep. Busyness fills a schedule, but it fractures a family. It robs us of joy.

The antidote to busyness is balance. Finding balance begins with an honest conversation with God. Ask him, "God, why am I busy? What does busyness mean in my life? What does it mean in my relationship to you? Why am I so driven? Why are these tasks more important to me than people and relationships? What does this busyness represent?" And God will show you.

Once you've had a heart-to-heart with God about why you are so driven, recognize the brevity of life and slow down the pace. My friend Lynnda, who moves slowly and gracefully through her very full life, told me:

> I am grateful for the faces who join us around our table of daily life—whether family, neighbors, or friends. Our lives are filled to the brim and overflowing with the richness of relationships; the bond of love that comes from walking in the way of faith with a determination to live deep instead of fast. Peace instead of the rat race.

Lynnda understands the truths of James 4:14, "How do you know what your life will be like tomorrow? Your life is like the morning fog—it's here a little while, then it's gone" (NLT), and Job 7:7, "My life is but a breath" (TLB). These verses teach us that time is life and life is short. Some might conclude that the brevity of life requires us to move *fast* in response, to make sure we cram it all in before we die. But Lynnda has concluded that *because* life is short, every season must be savored slowly and actually enjoyed.

Of course, every season of life has limitations, as well as unique opportunities, whether you have toddlers at home, an empty nest, a full-time job, or health concerns related to age. Yet we go through life acting as if life is not changing at all. Ecclesiastes 3:1 says, "Everything on earth has its own time and its own season" (CEV). In truth, we need to be constantly adjusting our schedule and priorities based on the season of life we're in. Part of being balanced is knowing what season of life you're in and adjusting for it.

My favorite movies of all time are the Lord of the Rings Trilogy—I love the pageantry, the heroism, the grand themes of good against evil, and the wisdom of one of the main characters, Gandalf the Grey. When another character complains that he wishes these bad times had not come when they did, Gandalf responds with these words: "So do all who live to see such times. But that is not for them to decide. All we have to decide is what to do with the time that is given us."[4]

At the end of your life, will you be pleased with the decisions you made about the time that was given to you? More importantly, will God be pleased? The key is to yield control of our brief span of time to him daily, keeping in mind that depth, not speed, is the truest measure of a balanced life.

Psalm 31:15, "Hour by hour I place my days in your hand" (Message), is a verse that will keep you centered and focused on using your time wisely in the middle of calendars, to-do lists, and deadlines, thus nurturing joy in your soul.

Practice Acceptance

Another true confession: I am a perfectionist. It's not something I'm proud of, but I have jokingly said that I am a card-carrying member of the Perfectionists Club of America. I expect perfection from myself and others, and from the world I live in—which means I'm always setting myself up for disappointment.

I want my hair to look just right—and yet it never curls the same way twice. I precisely follow the manufacturer's directions for washing a new shirt, and it shrinks the first time I wash it. I go to church, and there's a typo in the song lyrics on the screen. And I get really upset because things are not, well, *perfect*.

I've been known to ask out loud, "Why is perfection so difficult?" Is it any wonder I get a few raised eyebrows in response? The answer to my question is simple. Perfection is not difficult. It's *impossible*. It's impossible because of what happened in Genesis 3. When Adam and Eve decided to eat the fruit off that tree so they could be like God, they unleashed a curse on our world. The world doesn't understand it. They call it Murphy's Law: If anything can go wrong, it will. They think it's cute and clever, but it's really Genesis 3 in action.

Perfectionism has its roots firmly planted not only in Genesis 3 but also in the environment we grew up in. Often a hard-to-please parent, family member, or highly respected teacher or coach can seriously damage our developing sense of self, causing us to carry around their "voice" in our heads as an inner critic.

How about you? Does your desire for perfection significantly interfere with your job or your ability to achieve your goals? Does it get in the way of developing deep relationships? Perfectionism's reach extends to eating disorders and anxiety disorders. It's nasty. Have you discovered that chasing after perfection robs you of joy and peace?

Richard Carlson writes, "I've yet to meet an absolute perfectionist whose life was filled with inner peace. The need for perfection and the desire for inner tranquility conflict with each other."[5]

What a relief it was for me to realize a few years ago that my desire for perfection in and of itself is not wrong. We were made for it! We were made for perfect bodies. We were made for perfect relationships. We were made for perfect minds. We were made to live forever. Something deep inside us calls out for what was lost, so we keep reaching for it, keep trying to find that perfection our souls long for.

So it's not wrong to long for perfection; it's just wrong to expect it on earth. It isn't found here. There truly is *something* wrong with *everything*. That's not just me, an Eeyore, talking. It's recognizing the fact that we live under the curse. Perfection will only come when God creates the new heaven and the new earth and paradise is restored. Paradise was lost in Genesis 3. But in Revelation 21 it is restored. When that prophecy is fulfilled, all we long for will be restored to us. God tells us he will "wipe every tear from their eyes. There will be no more death or mourning or crying or pain. . . . 'I am making everything new!'" (Rev. 21:4–5).

> *It's not wrong to long for perfection; it's just wrong to expect it on earth.*

That means no more living under the curse. It means hair that curls properly every time. Song lyrics with no typos. Conversations with no misunderstandings. It means no more relationships that go sour. No more mental illness. No more bodies that don't work right. No more cancer. Everything that has been broken will be restored. That's a reason for joy.

The antidote to perfectionism is acceptance—acceptance of our earthly imperfections because we are focused on the day when imperfection will be no more. If I try to experience perfection here on earth, I will come up short every time. If I keep looking for perfection within myself, I will kill the joy in me. You and I need to fire our inner critic! When I accept myself as I am instead of who I wish I was, when I accept those around me as they are, not as I wish they were, when I accept the world as it is, not as I wish it was, my joy in today as well as my hope for tomorrow can grow.

Fighting for Joy

I asked you at the beginning of this section how badly you want to experience joy in your life and if you are willing to fight for it. For joy to become a reality, you must fight against the heart attitudes of legalism, worry, workaholism, and perfectionism and instead nurture grace, trust, balance, and acceptance. It won't come without a struggle, but nothing worthwhile ever does. Once you and I become adept at nurturing joy in ourselves, we will find delight in nurturing it in others as well.

—— PRAYER ——

Father, it's overwhelming to see how I have allowed criticism and perfectionism, anxiety, doubt, and busyness to take root in my heart and crowd out joy. God, may I instead become a person of grace and trust, someone who reflects your joy for others to see. It's impossible for me to do that by myself. Go deep inside me and do your work. Change me so that I become a joyful person. In Jesus's name I pray, amen.

FOR REFLECTION ___
AND APPLICATION

1. What are the ways you kill joy in yourself?

2. Choose one way—grace, trust, balance, acceptance—
   and ask God to help you focus on building that joyful
   response in your life this week.

EIGHT

Nurturing Joy in Others

But what happens when we live God's way? He brings gifts into our lives, much the same way that fruit appears in an orchard—things like affection for others, exuberance about life, serenity. We develop a willingness to stick with things, a sense of compassion in the heart, and a conviction that a basic holiness permeates things and people. We find ourselves involved in loyal commitments.

Galatians 5:22 Message

There is more hunger for love and appreciation in this world than for bread.

Mother Teresa of Calcutta

Rick and I had terrible struggles in our first years of marriage that started right out of the gate—on our honeymoon. There were a variety of reasons, but one unfortunate incident created a huge wound. We were driving through Vancouver, Canada, and Rick looked at me and said very sweetly, tentatively, "I have this idea. I thought that maybe we could create a book together in which we record all the special things that happen to us in our years of marriage. The special places we went. Special events. Maybe take some pictures. So when we're an old married couple sitting on the porch in our rocking chairs, we can look back and see what a great life we had together."

I don't know why, but I was in a perverse mood that day, and I responded, "I think that's a terrible idea!" His face crumpled with disappointment and embarrassment. I don't remember what happened next—maybe the shame I still feel at destroying my new husband's offering of love has wiped out my memories—but I had crushed him! Here he had offered something so thoughtful and so not-mannish-at-all, and I took it and ground it into the dirt. It was a moment of pure meanness.

It took Rick twenty years, but he got me back!

One Christmas I decided Rick needed a new barbecue. Notice I said, "I decided." We had a barbecue that was so badly broken that only Rick could figure out how to light it without incinerating himself. I thought, *I can't even send the kids out to turn it on before Rick gets home because it'll burn them up!*

A warehouse store was going out of business, and I bought this beautiful, smokin'-hot barbecue for him. Not only was it an incredible barbecue with lots of bells and whistles, but it was also cheap! I was beside myself with excitement to know I had an extra-special gift for him that Christmas. I put it out in the garage with a sheet over it until the big reveal on Christmas morning.

On Christmas Day, we had all the extended family over and the house was full of people. Everybody knew I had a special gift for Rick, so at the very end of opening presents, we all filed out to the garage. Somebody had a video camera ready to capture the joy he was going to experience. I couldn't wait for Rick to look under the sheet and see the barbecue.

"What is it?" he asked, lifting the sheet.

"It's a barbecue!" I said with forced cheerfulness and a slight note of desperation, dimly aware that the "big" moment was about to end in disaster.

He took one look at it and said, "I don't need a barbecue." And my Christmas hopes and dreams hit the ground.

Just so you don't judge Rick too harshly, I should tell you that he had been dropping hints for months about getting satellite TV. So he was super-excited, anticipating the large box under the sheet to hold a satellite dish. When he pulled the sheet off and it was a barbecue, it didn't quite hit the right note. I barely made it up to the bedroom, where I sobbed, hit my pillow, and said all kinds of bad words about him. I was humiliated in front of everybody, and I was so disappointed. Not only was my gift rejected, but I was stuck with the stupid barbecue because the store had since closed! (My father-in-law, Rick's dad, was so sweet. He said, "You know, I've been needing a new barbecue." And he bought it from me that day, and it sat unused on his patio until he died two years later.)

Just so you know the end of the story—we didn't head for divorce court the next day. We had a LONG conversation that included tears, hugs, and reconciliation. The experience was definitely awkward and painful at the time, but it has become a family legend. "The Christmas

Barbecue" story never fails to elicit groans, laughter, and a lot of teasing.

As we saw in the last chapter, we each have habits—such as legalism, worry, busyness, and perfectionism—that instead of nurturing joy deep within us actually kill joy in us. Apparently, we want to share the misery with others, because rather than nurturing joy in others, we often kill the joy in them that God wants them to have. I killed joy in Rick; he killed joy in me. I don't want to do that anymore. I'll bet you don't either.

An ancient philosopher, Philo of Alexandria, said, "Be kind. Everyone you meet is fighting a hard battle." How would your daily interactions change if you viewed people through that lens? If you knew that every person you encounter—family member, friend, co-worker, neighbor, stranger—has a hidden sorrow, wouldn't it transform your attitude toward them? What if you saw one of your primary purposes in life as nurturing joy in others? Do you think it would affect the level of joy *you* experience?

Let's take a look at four ways we can be a part of nurturing joy in those around us—in other words, ways we can invite others to experience the joy we've discovered.

Believe the Best about Others

Cynicism is rampant in our culture. We've gotten used to the record-setting professional athlete who, it turns out, was using performance-enhancing drugs. We've grown accustomed to the vocal politician who stands up for family values and is visiting prostitutes, or the well-respected community leader who is caught padding expense accounts.

We've come to expect that people aren't what they say they are and always have an angle.

Sarcastic, cynical humor reigns on sitcoms and news shows; the meaner the better. It's funny on TV, but it's devastating in real life.

Maybe part of our cynicism comes from knowing that we're not always totally up front with *our* motives. We're often out to work a situation in our favor too. As a result, we not only assume the worst in others, but we also act as if we know the motivation behind everything they do.

First Corinthians 13:7 says, "If you love someone you will be loyal to him no matter what the cost. You will always believe in him, always expect the best of him, and always stand your ground in defending him" (TLB).

Did you get that? Always expect the best, not the worst. What a refreshing response to believe in others rather than always looking for the hidden motive. If a co-worker schedules a meeting on a day you were hoping to take off, don't assume he scheduled it just to annoy you. Assume he didn't realize you would be gone and might be willing to change the day so you can attend. If you hear a rumor at church that a friend criticized you, assume the best in that person and try to find out the truth rather than assuming the rumor is true.

Assuming the best in others keeps us from assigning motives to someone's behavior. I'm sharing with you some of my life mottoes, and here's one of the best (ignore the grammar and concentrate on the point): "Never assume nothin' about nobody." This is a "Relationships 101" principle, because we can't even figure out our own motives let alone someone else's!

In C. S. Lewis's classic book *The Screwtape Letters*, a senior devil, Screwtape, is instructing a junior devil,

Wormwood, in how to bring division between a son and his mother, who live in the same home. Screwtape encourages Wormwood to capitalize on irritating behaviors between the two housemates by making them think the other person is *trying* to be annoying.

"When two humans have lived together for many years, it usually happens that each has tones of voice and expressions of face which are almost unendurably irritating to the other," Screwtape writes. The devil's job is to let the son assume that his mother *knows* how annoying a certain habit is and does it to annoy. "If you know your job, he will not notice the immense improbability of the assumption."[1]

Assuming that someone is doing something just to inconvenience you or because he or she does not value you is always dangerous to relationships and to joy.

"A joyful heart is good medicine," we read in Proverbs 17:22 (GW). If you want to give a friend a dose of good medicine, believe she has good motives. Believe what he says. Believe they want the best for you too. It will fill their heart with joy.

Offer Nonjudgmental Love

If you're a perfectionist with yourself, you're probably also somebody who criticizes other people. Those two tend to go together. Because you're not happy with yourself, you're not happy with others.

Some of us feel duty-bound to point out to other people their imperfections. Then we expect them to be grateful for it, as if they'll say, "Oh, thank you! I was waiting for you to tell me about that flaw today!" Even worse, we point out someone's imperfections to *other* people, falling into the trap of gossip and judgment.

When we criticize someone, it has a lot more to do with our need to be critical than with their imperfections or differences. And when we are critical of another person, we are missing the beauty in them and in our relationship with them. We destroy the delicate seedling of joy that is trying to take root in their heart. In Romans 2:1, we read, "Every time you criticize someone, you condemn yourself. It takes one to know one. Judgmental criticism of others is a well-known way of escaping detection in your own crimes and misdemeanors" (Message).

A few years ago, Rick sat down with me and said something that sobered me up fast. He said, "Kay, I don't think you like me."

I said, "What? Of course I like you! What do you mean I don't like you?"

He said, "You're always picking on me. You criticize how my shirt is tucked in or not tucked in. You tell me whether this color goes with that color. You tell me my hair is sticking up, and you smooth it down like I'm six years old. You treat me like a child. No matter what my opinion is, you have something to say about it. You just pick at me all the time."

My first response was, "No way! I don't do that! I do not behave like that."

And he said, "Yes, you really do. I know you love me, but I'm not sure you like me anymore."

So I went back to the Lord that night and I said, "God, you've got to help me here. Because I have the feeling he's right. And this is really sad and ugly."

The Lord reminded me of this image from the Bible: "If you keep on biting and devouring each other, watch out or you will be destroyed by each other" (Gal. 5:15). Then he gave me a picture of Rick as a cardboard cutout—and I was Ms. Pac-Man. I kept coming up to Rick and taking a bite out of him. Gobble, gobble. I took little pieces of him over and over. I could see that if I kept doing that, I was going to destroy him. I was going to destroy the love between us. I was going to kill our joy by this constant gobble, gobble, gobble!

Is there someone in your life you keep picking at? I'm not talking about big things. I mean little bites, constantly. The Bible says in Luke 6:37, "Don't pick on people, jump on their failures, criticize their faults—unless, of course, you want the same treatment. Don't condemn those who are down; that hardness can boomerang. Be easy on people; you'll find life a lot easier" (Message). How much clearer does Scripture have to be before we see that we kill joy when we can't offer others nonjudgmental love?

You might be thinking, I "pick" on her because she has some major flaws and weaknesses and I know how to help her! It's absurd to think that picking on someone—being overly critical and judgmental—will make them change, yet we do it constantly. It's futile, my friends. I recently found this anonymous riff on Reinhold Niebuhr's famous serenity prayer: "God, grant me the serenity to accept the people I cannot change, the courage to change the one I can, and the wisdom to know it's me."

Philippians 4:8 says, "Keep your thoughts on whatever is right or deserves praise: things that are true, honorable, fair, pure, acceptable, or commendable" (GW).

Think of the person closest to you. How much of that person is good and worthy and acceptable and wonderful? You might say, "Ninety percent! There's only ten percent of him that drives me crazy." Or you might say, "Fifty-fifty. It's hard to see the good in her sometimes."

As you apply this Scripture, where do you think you need to put the emphasis in your thinking about that person? On the part that is irritating, frustrating, immature, and weak? Or on the part that is awesome, the part that is worthy of honor and commendation and respect? If you put all your attention on the negative, you are creating a miserable relationship.

It doesn't matter what the percentage is. Where you put your focus and your energy is going to determine how successful that relationship is. Every relationship you and I have would improve 100 percent if we would apply this, if we would put our focus on what's right, on what's good, on what's worthy of respect in that person. Yes, there's brokenness, immaturity, things that need to change. But until we focus first on what is good, we will not know joy in that relationship.

Remember, nothing will restore joy in another person's heart faster than the words, "I accept you as you are."

Empathize with Others' Feelings

Have you ever said, "It's cold in here!" and the other person responded, "No, it's not." Or told somebody, "I'm feeling discouraged," and she replied, "Don't be silly! You shouldn't feel that way." You weren't looking for a lecture. You were looking for a listening ear and a little kindness.

Instead of empathizing with other people's feelings, many times we minimize their feelings or try to diagnose what's "wrong" with them. Just as we have a hard time figuring out our own motives, we don't always know our own feelings. But we turn into Dr. Phil when it comes to our family members and best friends, telling them what they're thinking and feeling—or what they *should* be thinking and feeling.

Proverbs 14:10 says, "Each heart knows its own bitterness, and no one else can fully share its joy" (NLT). Only God knows what another person is thinking or feeling, and we are arrogant when we assume that we do. This robs their joy.

Instead, we need to empathize with each other and listen to the feelings before we start handing out advice or moving into action. Jesus was touched by the sadness, suffering, and distress of those he ministered to, and the Bible frequently comments that his heart was full of compassion in response.

In Luke 7:11–17, Jesus encounters a widow whose only son has just died. Her grief was shattering and her future was bleak because, as a widow, she was now completely alone with no son to care for her in her old age. Jesus could have swept by her as just one more hurting person or simply waved his hand from a distance and brought her son back to life. But verse 13 says, "When Jesus saw her, his heart broke. He said to her, 'Don't cry'" (Message). He felt what she felt, grieved as she grieved, and *then* he went into action to restore life to her dead son.

We read in 1 Peter 3:8, "Finally, all of you should be of one mind. Sympathize with each other. Love each other as brothers and sisters. Be tenderhearted, and keep a humble attitude" (NLT).

You show that you love someone when you listen to them and join in their celebration or tears, recognizing that you do not know their heart the way God does. You help restore joy to their heart when you validate their feelings. Validation doesn't mean you approve of what somebody says or even that you agree with it. You might be sitting there thinking, *This is nuts! I've never heard of anything so bizarre!* But those should never be the first words out of your mouth. In fact, if you're famous for telling people exactly what you think, don't be surprised if fewer and fewer people seek you out to process their feelings—instead of nurturing joy in others, it's possible you're building a reputation for being a joy killer.

Validation just says, "I hear you. I hear what you're saying; I receive your feelings."

What a gift we give to each other when we receive into our hands and our hearts somebody else's feelings. People are dying to be listened to. People are dying to be able to pour out their hearts and not be judged, not be told they're crazy, not be told their feelings don't matter. At Saddleback, sometimes we repeat this sentence together as a congregation: "I'm broken, but I'm not crazy." You can sense the release and relief that washes over those gathered as we affirm this truth to one another.

One of the best things about going to a therapist (I have been through a lot of therapy in my life, and I highly recommend it!) is having a place where someone just listens. Granted, they're paid to listen, but it's such a relief to pour out my anxieties, confusion, and hurts and have someone just receive those words.

> *What a gift we give to each other when we receive into our hands and our hearts somebody else's feelings.*

There are SO many lonely people who ache to be listened to, validated, and empathized with. Psalm 69:20 says, "I'm broken by their taunts, flat on my face, reduced to a nothing.

I looked in vain for one friendly face. Not one. I couldn't find one shoulder to cry on" (Message).

We don't have enough money for all the therapy we need, and we never will. So let's be listeners for each other. Let's hold each other's hearts in our hands for just a few moments and validate each other's significance. Let's comfort each other with the comfort God has given to us (2 Cor. 1:4–8). Taylor Caldwell said, "[Man's] real need, his most terrible need, is for someone to listen to him, not as a 'patient,' but as a human soul."[2]

Is there someone in your life who often tells you that you don't listen? You might disagree, but if they feel you're not listening, there's a good chance you're not. Ask yourself these questions: *What's it like to be on the other side of me? What does everybody around me experience from me? Do I make people defensive by demanding they give an explanation for their feelings, or am I compassionate about others' feelings?* This week make it a point to let that person pour out their heart without being judgmental or critical. Just listen.

Ephesians 4:32 says, "Become useful and helpful and kind to one another, tenderhearted (compassionate, understanding, loving-hearted), forgiving one another [readily and freely], as God in Christ forgave you" (AMP).

When we listen to others with compassion, without assuming we know what they are thinking or feeling, without judging or criticizing, we add joy to their lives.

Appreciate Others' Efforts

I can summarize this point in two words: *thank you!* It's amazing how far those two little words will go in filling someone else's heart with joy. As we seek to nurture joy in others, we can help it bloom in them by thanking them for service they have given and for efforts they have made to grow and change.

The apostle Paul was a master at showing appreciation. Every letter he wrote is full of personal greetings and words of affirmation for those who helped him in any way: "I thank God for you," "I thank my God upon every remembrance of you," "I remember the help you gave from the first day you believed."

While Paul was grateful, one of the mistakes we make in this area is that we approach relationships with a sense of *you owe me.* When you operate from that place of entitlement, it turns everything that somebody gives to you as an offering of love into a repayment of a debt. You end up thinking, *Why should I thank you for doing that? That's what you're supposed to do.*

And joy is nowhere to be found because nothing is received as a gift. Nothing is received in love. The other person always has the feeling that he can never give you enough compared to all you feel you've done for him. The debt is never repaid. This is a no-win situation in a relationship; you feel cheated and your loved one feels used. Joy evaporates.

Another way to nurture joy in a friend is to express delight with the emotional or spiritual growth we see taking place in their life. Unfortunately, we miss this opportunity because we think the other person isn't changing as fast as they should. She hasn't grown enough. He hasn't learned enough. We think, *I don't want to applaud that effort because then they'll think they don't need to change more. They'll stop trying.*

My baby granddaughter, Claire, is just learning to smile and coo. How stupid it would be for me to expect her to start talking tomorrow! She can't, and, moreover, she shouldn't. She's doing exactly what she should be doing at this age. No matter how many hours I stand over her crib urging her to say, "Hi, Grammy!" it isn't going to happen until the time is right. We're foolish when we berate others to "grow faster" emotionally or spiritually; growth is slow and incremental. Claire needs my affirmation that her coos are lovely and sweet and that I appreciate each one. As she grows, each round of enthusiastic applause for her efforts will make her want to keep trying.

Again, the apostle Paul sets an example for us to follow. It seems as though he spent the bulk of his ministry encouraging others to grow up in Christ, writing beautiful words of encouragement, affirmation, and applause: "I so want to be there . . . and watch you grow stronger right before my eyes"; "Just like a mother in childbirth, I feel the same kind of pain for you until Christ's nature is formed in you"; "So, my dear brothers and sisters, be strong and steady." He spoke like a loving father to people at times, giving words of correction and rebuke when necessary, but his appreciation of their efforts to grow never wavered.

Paul simply reflected *his* Father's patience and affirmation of him and then passed them on to those coming up behind him. Are you convinced that God is pleased with your efforts, even as he wants you to keep changing and growing? If you are, you'll find it easier to be patient with the baby steps your friends and family are taking. Change is hard enough as it is. Without encouragement, it can feel impossible.

Most of the people around you are trying hard to make changes in their lives. Receiving applause from someone who notices their efforts will give them a joy that will encourage them even more.

Change Is Possible

In the last two chapters, we've looked at ways we fail to nurture joy in ourselves and others: legalism, worry, workaholism, perfectionism, cynicism, criticism, selfishness, and ingratitude. If those attitudes are in you, you will not experience joy.

Granted, you can make some minor changes that might make you happier and improve your personal relationships, but those changes won't necessarily lead to joy. Joy is not a surface attitude adjustment but a settled assurance about God, a quiet confidence in God, and a determined choice to praise him in every situation. Joy takes the long view of life rather than the short view, always looking ahead to better things. Only those who are convinced that God is in control of the future can yield control to others now. Those who believe God will eventually make all things right can afford to wait patiently now. Those who have placed their soul's well-being in the care of a gracious God can smile at days yet to come.

Choosing to cultivate grace, trust, balance, acceptance, positive thoughts about others, nonjudgmental love, empathy, and appreciation will allow joy to grow in you, creating life-altering transformation at the core of who you are.

One last word as we talk about changing and growing in our heart-responses. If you were willing to make a true confession, some of you would have to admit that you're not feeling very good right now. You've recognized the broken, destructive ways you kill joy in yourself and the people around you, but instead of being willing to change, you've convinced yourself of a lie: "That's just the way I am. I've always been this way, and everybody knows it. I can't change. When I'm under stress, I can't help the way I respond. You know where I've come from; just cut me some slack."

May I gently suggest that your attitude reveals one or a combination of four possible problems: (1) You have been severely wounded throughout your life, and your rough language, attitudes, and behavior are your attempt to protect yourself from vulnerability; (2) you have tried to change on numerous occasions and failed miserably, and any talk of change just takes you to that place of hopelessness; (3) you are angry and bitter and in an active state of rebellion against God's seemingly impossible demands; or (4) you simply have not yet allowed Christ's love to go deeply enough into the soil of your heart to create transformation of the old you into the new you (1 Cor. 5:7).

We think change happens when God drives us with a whip, when actually the most lasting change happens as we draw close to his heart of compassion and let him embrace us. Just as Jesus's heart was broken for the suffering of the widow in Luke 7, his heart suffers for your suffering. He calls you to come and be transformed in the context of his faithful, unshakable love for you. You don't need to be afraid anymore. Real change is possible. You and I truly can become people of joy, nurturing it in ourselves and in the lives of those we dearly love.

—— **PRAYER** ——

God, I want to be someone who offers forgiveness, encouragement, and nonjudgmental love to others. I want to be someone who listens well, someone who assumes the best about people and doesn't judge their motives. I need help to do this because it does not come naturally to me. Work through me to build joy in others. In Jesus's name, amen.

FOR REFLECTION AND APPLICATION

1. Can you think of ways you've killed joy in the lives of others? Which is most common for you—cynicism, criticism, selfishness, or ingratitude?

2. Ask God to help you be a conduit for joy this week.

JOY Is A Choice of My Behavior

PART 4

Ways to Choose Joy Daily

s March 20 circled in red on your calendar? If not, it should be—it's the International Day of Happiness! In case you missed its beginnings, it was created by the United Nations General Assembly in 2012 in response to a suggestion by the prime minister of Bhutan, who thought happiness deserved a day all to itself. You know how these things go—first a special day is set aside, then somebody says, "Well, we probably ought to research which countries are the happiest," and before you know it, a study is commissioned, and an annual report ranking the overall happiness levels of 156 countries is issued! Of course, experts can quibble with each other all day over what metrics should be used to measure happiness, but this particular study focuses on six variables of well-being: income, freedom, trust, healthy life expectancy, social support, and generosity.[1]

According to the World Happiness Report for 2019, Americans are not happy people—and we're getting unhappier. The United States is ranked 19th, down a spot from 2018 and down five spots from 2017.

A CNN article on the report stated that, "Except for its 10th place ranking for income, the US doesn't rank in the top 10 on measures that make up a happy country in the UN report. They include 12th place for generosity, 37th place for social support, 61st place for freedom and 42nd place for corruption."[2]

Coauthor of the report and director of the Sustainable Development Solutions Network Jeffrey Sachs names addiction as partly to blame. "This year's report provides sobering evidence of how addictions are causing considerable unhappiness and depression in the US." In a press release, he said, "Addictions come in many forms, from substance abuse to gambling to digital media. The compulsive pursuit of substance abuse and addictive behaviors is causing severe unhappiness."[3]

A "happiness" report like this one can leave us feeling a bit hopeless—there's certainly no shortage of bad news. How can average people find life meaningful, worthwhile, and joyful? How do we turn all the principles, Scripture passages, and ideas we've been looking at from the theoretical to the practical? How do we make joy a choice of our behavior? This section looks at ways we can choose joy on a daily basis, regardless of what is going on around us.

NINE

Getting Back to Basics

You know me inside and out,
   you know every bone in my body;
You know exactly how I was made, bit by bit,
   how I was sculpted from nothing
into something.

Psalm 139:15–16 Message

We can hug our hurts and make a shrine out of our sorrows or we can offer them to God as a sacrifice of praise. The choice is ours.

Richard Exley

We know that Jesus was a man of joy and a man of sorrows. His life gives us permission to seek a life of joy for ourselves. We also know that joy is a conviction of our minds, as truth begins to transform us over time, as well as an attitude of our hearts, as we cultivate appropriate responses to trials.

Now is the time for doing. Are you going to read this book and think, *Yeah, that's a good point. Someday I might get around to that?* Or are you going to be a doer of God's Word, moving out of the theoretical into the practical? Remember that joy is not about happy feelings. It's a settled assurance *about* God. A quiet confidence *in* God. And a determined choice to give our praise *to* God in all things. It means choosing joy again and again and again in the ups and downs, ins and outs of daily life. And it starts with getting back to the basics.

What Matters Most: Take Care of Yourself

As we've already touched on, we talk a lot about our priorities and how we spend our time. I honestly believe the words *priorities* and *guilt* can be used interchangeably for many of us. In fact, one of our favorite (but really sick) pastimes is to make a list of the priorities in our lives—God, family, job, friends, ministry, hobbies, etc.—and then torture ourselves by fretting over the ways we are doing a lousy job in each area! Why do we do this to ourselves? It's incredibly dysfunctional and unhealthy, as well as completely unhelpful.

One of the items on your priority list matters more than all the others, but I'm willing to bet this item isn't even ON the priority list for most of you. For those of you who were raised in church, it may seem selfish and downright unbiblical to you at first, but, my friends, your first priority should be you. *You matter.* Your thoughts matter, your opinions matter, your hurts and wounds matter, your dreams and goals matter. You matter to God. You matter to your family. When you understand this, you can focus on who you are in Christ and where you need to grow. Soon the truth that you matter will become a foundation for joy.

I believe taking care of yourself—nourishing your body, soul, and spirit—may be *the key* to choosing joy daily. To get back to the basics, start by simplifying your life. I enjoy home organization and life management books, but that's not what I have in mind when I say you need to simplify your life. Simplifying your life is not about decluttering your closets or car or getting rid of junk; it's not about eliminating activities in your schedule so you can do more. Simplifying means focusing on who you are physically, emotionally, and spiritually so that who you are can come alive, ready to receive joy and give joy.

You and I are involved—overinvolved—in a zillion activities. When we are overinvolved in things that may not matter even five years from now, we leave no time for ourselves. We leave no time to nourish ourselves physically and emotionally and spiritually. And when we don't nourish ourselves, the little fire that burns inside us, that zeal and passion that get us up in the morning and push us back into the world every day, starts to go out. From that place of coldness, it's extremely difficult to experience joy. It's extremely difficult to nurture joy in anyone else because our own inner fire has gone dead. Our souls become barren, parched, and dry.

You matter to God. You matter to your family. When you understand this, you can focus on who you are in Christ and where you need to grow.

In case you haven't figured it out by now, let me share a secret with you: Nobody's going to take care of you. I don't mean that in a cynical way. I don't mean that in a bash-on-spouse, bash-on-parents, bash-on-children way. I just mean that at the end of the day no one is going to do the three things for you that we're going to look at next. Nobody can. That's why I live by this motto: Control the controllables and leave the uncontrollables to God. So many variables factor into what my life looks like on a daily basis; some of them are within my control, but many are not. You and I must accept responsibility for controlling what we can and leave the rest to God's sovereignty. I have chosen to control the following three aspects of my life, thus nourishing myself.

Physical Aspect

Rick and I recently visited the brain surgeon at UCLA who operated on our daughter-in-love, Jaime, several years ago. As we chatted with him in the hall, we told him about the Daniel Plan, a year-long program we've developed in our church to help people eat right and stay physically fit. (You can find out more about it at www.danielplan.com.) The doctor got really excited and said, "Do you know that 80 percent of the people who are in the hospital today are there because of lifestyle choices? If Christians started taking more responsibility for their lifestyle choices, we could drastically improve the health of our nation!"

Eighty percent. That's staggering! Hospitals are filled with people like you and me who make poor nutritional and fitness choices and then end up with diabetes, heart disease, high blood pressure, and high cholesterol.

I realize this is a sensitive subject, but it's one worth exploring thoroughly. Our physical choices are not a side issue in our life with God. Paul says in 1 Corinthians 6:19–20:

Or didn't you realize that your body is a sacred place, the place of the Holy Spirit? Don't you see that you can't live however you please, squandering what God paid such a high price for? The physical part of you is not some piece of property belonging to the spiritual part of you. God owns the whole works. So let people see God in and through your body. (Message)

You have no other way than through your physical body to interact with or minister God's grace to fellow human beings. So if our bodies are falling apart—weak, tired, out of energy—and are not operating at optimal speed because we're not taking care of ourselves, we will shortchange what God can do through us.

It's taken me a while to come to this conclusion, but I've discovered that I'm in total control over what goes in my mouth. Nobody force-feeds me. Nobody holds me down. Nobody makes me eat anything I don't want to eat. I eat what I choose to eat. It's just that I have a problem (maybe you do too) with an overactive right arm. My overactive arm is constantly shoveling things into my mouth. But that's my responsibility. I can't blame anybody else. I can't blame my genes. I can't blame anything other than an arm that is on the constant move to put food in my face.

Study after study shows that those who are the most active have fewer lifestyle-based illnesses. Even Dr. Mehmet Oz has said that the best antiaging secret is to do everything possible to keep yourself from getting frail.[1] Thirty minutes a day of some sort of activity is all that is needed to stave off those extra pounds and the ever-increasing toll of aging bones and muscles.

Of course, I'm speaking in generalities; this is a broad topic with thousands of books, websites, and other resources that go into great detail about health and fitness. I don't mean to sound insensitive to health issues that are genetic, caused by accidents, or seemingly come from out of nowhere. I'm talking to those of us who could—but don't usually choose to—control what we eat, how active we are, how much we sleep, and how fit we are.

Our body is one thing we can learn to take care of so that we can find joy in fulfilling what God asks us to do.

Emotional Aspect

Each of us has been wounded by our families, our friends, circumstances we brought on ourselves, as well as things beyond our personal choices. Some of the wounds have left us broken, discouraged, and damaged. But to experience joy daily, we need to take responsibility for how emotionally strong and healthy we are in spite of our hurts. Remember my motto: Control the controllables and leave the uncontrollables to God.

I know what it's like to hurt. Some wounds have healed enough to just leave scars, but other wounds are as fresh today as the day they were inflicted. But what am I going to do about it? It's easy to whine. It takes courage to begin to change, to find ways to heal.

Some of our broken places require the care, comfort, and counsel of wise people who can gently but firmly guide us back to emotional health. Early in our marriage, when conflict, differences, and past hurts were threatening to destroy our relationship, Rick and I decided we needed professional counseling to help us build a strong marriage. We didn't have the money to pay for counseling—we were college students— but we found a way. Throughout our years together, we have made that decision multiple times and are so grateful for all we have learned from godly professionals who invested in our emotional health.

Don't avoid getting help for your stuck places. At Celebrate Recovery, our Christian twelve-step program, we say, "If you could have fixed it by now, you would have, but since you can't, you won't!" You might need professional counseling, as we did, and yes, professional counseling costs money, but there are many who offer their services on a sliding scale. Most churches have staff members who offer limited counseling, and some larger churches have trained lay counselors who work with individuals at no cost. Thousands of churches around the world offer Celebrate Recovery (www .celebraterecovery.com), and I guarantee you there's a chapter in a church near your home. There are free mental health services offered through state and local agencies, as well as numerous online support groups for every conceivable problem.

Unresolved emotional pain and brokenness can make choosing joy on a daily basis challenging. But remember, ultimately we must actively choose to do what we can to take care of ourselves emotionally.

On a lighter note, what do you do that pours life back into you emotionally? For me, playing the piano nourishes my inner soul. I'm not a great piano player, but when I play the piano, I express things I can't put into words, things I don't know how to articulate. Playing the piano taps into feelings and emotions deep inside me and allows me to create something of beauty that releases my emotions.

All of us need an outlet for creative expression and release. For you, it may be turning your garage into the perfect guy zone. It may be taking a cooking class or gardening. It may be needlework, playing a sport, or exercising. Your creative outlet is not just a *good thing*; *it's necessary for emotional health*.

You young moms and dads are probably screaming at me, "Yeah, maybe in ten years when I'm not up at all hours of the night with a baby or supervising my kids' home-work projects." I hear you—I really do—and I vividly recall that exhausting but delightful season of my life. Even if I couldn't remember it, I watch my own children live it out every week. This gentle push to nourish your inner life is meant to encourage, not discourage. You don't have to do anything big, but choose one small way that you can cherish yourself: read a chapter in a great book, visit one stimulat-ing (and uplifting) online community, walk the dog at sun-set, try a new recipe—whatever refreshes you. Remember two things: First, you matter! Second, control what you can control. God doesn't hold us responsible for things beyond our control.

For all of us—in every season of our lives—one important way to take responsibility for our emotional health is to do something creative, allowing our spirits to be nourished as we pour life back into them.

Spiritual Aspect

You are as close to God as you want to be. I am as close to God as I want to be. The Bible reassures us that God will never leave us or abandon us. He will never forsake us or walk away from us. So if there is distance in your walk with God, a sense of coolness, it's not because God has moved. God has not shifted locations. The Bible is clear: God has not lost any of his love or passion for you. Somewhere in your walk with him, you have allowed distance to occur. If you want to return to intimacy with God, it falls on your shoulders to do what it takes to get back to a place where you're feeling close to him.

Just as it's easier for me to blame my genes for the tendency to gain weight around my midsection than to be aware of what I'm eating and choose to be more active, and easier to blame the relational wounds I've received for my emotional immaturity than to intentionally seek wise counsel and guidance from spiritually mature people, it's far easier to blame God for distance between us and pull away from him than to do the things I know will restore closeness. The truth is that most of the time we don't want to control the controllables in our lives because to do so would dramatically increase the level of personal responsibility we must assume, and frankly, that's uncomfortable.

> *Simplifying your life means focusing on who you are physically, emotionally, and spiritually. If you want to choose joy daily, that's the place to start.*

Nobody determines in the morning whether I get up and spend time with God except me. Nobody determines how much I pray except me. Rick doesn't get to do that for me. I can't ask him to. I can't ask him to have faith for me. I can't ask him to surrender to God on my behalf. I can't ask him to place my hope in Christ. I have to do it. You have to do it.

If we want to be close to God and see our relationship with him develop and mature, we've got to grab the reins of our spiritual life and make those decisions of surrender, saying yes to God, trusting him, and putting his Word into practice. No one but us can make that happen.

So don't simplify your life so you can do more. Simplify your life so you can focus on what matters—and *you* are what matters. Simplifying your life means focusing on who you are physically, emotionally, and spiritually. If you want to choose joy daily, that's the place to start.

Getting to Know You: Look for a Joy Mentor

You and I are on a quest to develop some new habits; we want to become people who respond to life with joy, not sorrow. So we need to be around people who are already doing that and can reinforce these new habits in us.

John Ortberg, the author of *The Life You've Always Wanted*, suggests we find joy mentors: people who are a little farther down this joy road than we are. Find someone who seems to be a joyful person and get as close to them as you can. Observe them. Ask questions; find out how they got to the place of choosing to face life with joy. I'm not talking about someone who just has a great personality. I'm talking about a person who through life's ups and downs has developed a deep, settled assurance about God and his goodness, believes that ultimately everything will be all right, and repeatedly demonstrates a willingness to praise God in all things.

All of us need mature joy mentors as role models, but let me tell you about the sweetest joy mentors: children! Nobody has a better sense of humor than small children. Nobody. They will laugh at anything! You hit yourself on the head, they laugh. You make funny sounds, they laugh. You make strange faces, they laugh. *Again!* they demand. And they will beg you to do it again and again and again until you are exhausted. And if you ever laugh at something they do, forget about your to-do list because they will gleefully, repeatedly perform their action and expect you to laugh just as hard as they did for you—each time.

Small children are a joy factory! Because most have yet to experience the painful, harsher realities of this world, they laugh for no apparent reason; they crack themselves up! They're not embarrassed to have their food spurt out of their mouths while laughing. They don't care if they fall off their chairs laughing. They will roll around on the floor laughing. Even some of the most vulnerable children on the planet know how to laugh about something. Children provide the purest model for unabashed, uninhibited joy you can find.

Maybe you don't have kids in your life, or the ones you do have don't live near you. So how can you access one of these little joy mentors? Perhaps you can volunteer in the children's ministry at church or at a kids' recreation program. Be with your neighbor's kids. Smile at a toddler in a restaurant who is making happy sounds. Usually we frown at kids for making noise, and we squish the joy out of them. Don't squish the joy! It leaves fast enough. Enjoy the joy that little children have, because they are still aware that they were made to be joyful.

One more word about intentionally seeking to be around joyful people. We become like the people we hang out with, for good or for bad. Every parent knows this. That's why 1 Corinthians 15:33 ("Bad friends will ruin good habits" [NCV]) was one of the verses we had our children memorize at an early age!

If you are around sour, negative, depressed people all the time, you will begin to take on their attitudes. It just happens. Studies have shown that people who live with depressed people eventually experience symptoms of depression themselves. Of course, depression isn't contagious the way the flu is. It's an emotional virus that wears down the resilience of people who have it as well as those who are around it.

Don't misunderstand me and think I'm saying that if you are close to someone who is depressed you should avoid him or her. I'm just saying that you need to counterbalance those relationships with joyful people so that your own level of joy can increase.

Joy Conservation: Avoid Small Potatoes

It's not just the big things that rob us of joy but the hundreds of small irritations, minor disappointments, and pesky misunderstandings that pile up over the course of a day and manage to sour our mood. Even if we learn how to get a good handle on worry, perfectionism, cynicism, grace, forgiveness, and empathy, there are still countless ways for joy to disappear if we're not vigilant about our behavioral responses, our choices.

For instance, my desk at work faces a ground-floor window that looks out into the parking lot for the small office complex in which my office is located. Each building has a certain number of parking spaces allotted to it based on the square footage of the building. The building next to mine houses a busy medical practice, and the employees have evidently been instructed *not* to park near their building so that patients can park closer to their entrance. But instead of parking around the corner, where there are more spaces, their employees park in the spaces in front of *my* building! And since my window is only a few yards away from the parking lot, I have witnessed them parking in *our* spaces—including the ones directly in front of my door—every day for years. It didn't really bother me much until one day as I was getting into my car, one of their employees began to complain to me about how every once in a while people attending a meeting at my office park in THEIR parking places! Being conscious of my role as a representative of Jesus Christ, I held my tongue and politely said, "I'm sorry for the inconvenience; I'll remind them to carpool if possible."

Outwardly, I was calm, kind, and serene. But inwardly, I was a seething mass of anger and bitterness, and I badly wanted to heap sarcastic comments on this woman with her unjust complaints. I had to bite my tongue really hard to keep from saying, "Oh, I get it. It's okay for your employees to park in MY spaces every single day of the week, but you get your nose all out of joint when every once in a while someone coming to my office parks in one of YOUR spots? Isn't that just a teensy bit hypocritical?"

From that moment, I became maddeningly aware of the unfairness of the parking situation that unfolded every day *right in front of my eyes!* Watching the next-door office's employees park in my spaces began to get under my skin and cause my blood pressure to rise. What I used to not even notice became all I could see. Each morning I would grumble and fume and mutter to myself, and occasionally I would bring in my employees to commiserate with me as we watched their flagrantly disrespectful and unfair behavior.

I am embarrassed to admit how much time and emotional energy I gave to this small problem before I finally gave myself a good talking to. I reminded myself that, in the overall scheme of life, whether these people observed proper parking etiquette or not was simply not that important, and it absolutely wasn't worth the frustration, anger, bitterness, and loss of joy I was allowing myself to experience. Since I couldn't control THEM, I had to control ME.

I still can't always manage happy feelings toward my work neighbors, so my strategy for joy conservation is simple: I just lower the blinds! That way I'm not distracted by a situation that threatens to rob me of much-needed joy.

I know it sounds stupidly childish and immature—and it is. And some of you are disgusted or turned off by my inability to handle such a "small-potatoes" situation in a more mature manner. This is exactly the kind of incident that pundits have in mind when they tell us "not to sweat the small stuff."

But I'll bet if you were completely honest, you'd have to admit that you, too, have some "small-stuff" annoyances that rob you of joy over and over again. We end up judging each other about small stuff because what sends me up the wall might not faze you, and what drives you crazy might not bother me at all. But we all have our hot buttons—joy thieves—that cause us to focus on things that just don't matter and erode our sense of joy.

Would you be willing to take an inside look right now at your own daily life and see if there are any pesky joy thieves lurking around? Once you've identified the small ways that joy evaporates in your life, the BIG question is, what are you willing to do about it? As I've said throughout the book, ultimately, whether you experience joy or not is up to you. It comes down to what you choose to DO in every situation.

The Gift of Choice

What a gift God gives us when he gives us the opportunity to choose joy every day! Paul Tournier, noted Swiss psychiatrist, said, "Perhaps the most powerful and unused gift from

God is choice."[2] The key word in this quotation is *unused*. Many deny that they have choices in life, preferring instead to accept and enjoy misery. We get offended if anyone suggests such an idea to us, but a cold, hard look in the mirror reveals the truth. Aren't you ready to *use* this gift to choose to take hold of your inheritance of joy? I am.

—— PRAYER ——

Father, I acknowledge that it is up to me to choose joy in my life, to embrace the birthright you have given me. I pray for wisdom to know what I can and can't control. Help me to take care of myself physically, emotionally, and spiritually. I also pray for new eyes to see all that you are doing in my life. I want to be alert. I want to be grateful. And I ask that my enjoyment of life would be a part of my enjoyment of you. May I see new ways to praise you every day. In Jesus's name, amen.

___ FOR REFLECTION ___
AND APPLICATION

1. Make a list of three things you can control in your life and commit to controlling them. Next, make a list of three things you can't control—and "give" that list to God.

2. Think of the people you know who see the funny side of life. Make plans to be with them this week!

―――― TEN ――――

Loving and Laughing Together

I'll convert their weeping into laughter,
　　lavishing comfort, invading their grief with joy.

Jeremiah 31:13 Message

Do not hesitate to love and to love deeply. As you love deeply
the ground of your heart will be broken more and more, but
you will rejoice in the abundance of the fruit it will bear.

Henri Nouwen

One of my favorite guilty pastimes is to stand in line at the grocery store and read all the ridiculous, outrageous headlines on magazines and newspapers. "Three-headed baby born to London mother!" screams one. "US holding aliens in secret location in your city!" says another. But along with the goofy stories, there are other stories that tell us that relationships are the key to happiness. I'd like to reframe that idea: Relationships are one of the best opportunities we have to give and receive joy. We can't depend on them for happiness. But we can choose to find laughter, affection, pleasure, and hope in them. Sometimes all it takes is small changes in relationships to build a lasting foundation of joy.

God's Good Gifts: Rediscover Pleasure

As Americans, we are known for our exuberant pursuit of health, wealth, and happiness and a high emphasis on pleasure, but it wasn't always so.

Several hundred years ago, the Puritans fought against the excesses, corruption, and political influence that had begun to infiltrate the Church of England. After a back-and-forth struggle, they eventually lost power in England. Some migrated to America and colonized portions of the East Coast—we know them as the Pilgrims. Along with their heavy emphasis on hard work, honesty, and religious freedom, the Pilgrims also taught rigorous self-discipline and a strict adherence to biblical morality. In their efforts to maintain moral purity, they erected "fences" that put distance between them and anything that might tempt them to sin. Pleasure, happiness, enjoyment, laughter, and even smiling were suspect. Pleasure might lead to excess, and excess would lead to sin, and sin would lead to ruin and destruction.

And thus began a period in history of hypervigilance that found Christians avoiding anything that might even remotely smack of pleasure. This has had a powerful effect on the way Christians view the body and the senses in particular.

While it is true that pleasure out of control can lead to destructive hurts, habits, and hang-ups, there is no reason to automatically fear it or avoid it. Pleasure, in fact, comes from God.

We're told in 1 Timothy 6:17 to put our hope in God, "who richly provides us with everything for our enjoyment." Enjoyment and pleasure are synonyms. This verse might as well say, "Put your hope in God, who richly provides us with everything for our pleasure."

There are at least four philosophical approaches to our senses: (1) Deny them; this is taught in some forms of Buddhism. (2) Suppress them; this is asceticism. (3) Indulge them; this is hedonism. (4) Enjoy them; this is the biblical approach.

God has given you five senses. He didn't give you vision just to keep you from running into things. He didn't give you a sense of smell just so you can avoid toxic odors coming out of your refrigerator. He didn't give you touch just so you can avoid burning yourself on microwave popcorn. He didn't give us our senses merely so we can avoid pain but also so we take in pleasure. Our senses ease the pain of living in a broken world and actually open a door to joy.

Our senses ease the pain of living in a broken world and actually open a door to joy.

A few years ago, I received a gift certificate for a massage at a local spa that had just opened in a mall. I was so excited because I had no idea what to expect! While I waited for my massage, there were nuts and dried fruits to munch on. Cucumber had been added to a dispenser of ice water, and the delicate flavor intrigued my taste buds. When the masseuse took me to the massage room, the lights were low, and candles glowed invitingly. The sheets on the bed were deliciously soft to my skin, and her strong hands worked the oil, fragrant with eucalyptus and lavender, into my knotted back muscles. Gentle, melodic music played in the background, adding to the experience of relaxation. Sight, sound, touch, taste, and hearing were all engaged. For sixty minutes, the outside world ceased to exist for me! All I focused on was the release, rest, and pleasure that came from enjoying my senses.

We don't always have the luxury of a spa massage, but God invites us to take in pleasure every day.

Take a walk around your neighborhood one day this week, not for exercise but for pleasure. Stand in the sun for a few moments; close your eyes and let the warmth penetrate your skin. Take your shoes off in a nearby park and let the grass tickle your toes.

Take a bite of something yummy and roll it around in your mouth before you gulp it down. Try to figure out what makes it so tasty and delicious; savor the texture, the taste, the smell.

Walk outside tonight before you go to bed and just look at, listen to, and feel the night. Look at the majesty of the night sky, let the breeze touch your face, let your ears hear the night sounds.

When you get in bed, be aware of how the sheets feel. Rub your fingers over the softness of the blanket, smell the laundry detergent that perfumes your linens. Snuggle deep into your pillow and really feel the pleasure that comes from its comforting shape.

The good feelings that come when we rediscover pleasure sound suspiciously like happiness rather than joy. It's true that the pleasure is temporary, but the deliberate choice to turn our thoughts to the Giver of all good gifts causes happiness to step into joy's shoes.

Express Affection Extravagantly

When my kids were growing up, I tried to make it a practice to get up from whatever I was doing and establish physical contact with them as they walked in the door. It might have been a hug or a kiss for my daughter, Amy, or simply a touch on the shoulder for my boys, Josh and Matthew, when they got older and weren't so keen on bear hugs from Mom. Anything that established physical contact was a way of saying, "I love you." We can't underestimate the importance of physical affection in our relationships.

We're told in 1 Corinthians 13:13, "Love extravagantly" (Message). Are you an extravagant lover with your touch? Most of us dole out love in little pieces depending on how well the person who is supposed to love us actually loves us. If he is loving us well, we are more willing to love him extravagantly. If he is not loving us well, we get stingy with our love and therefore with our physical affection. We give it out carefully as if it is in short supply and needs to be hoarded.

You and I were made for connection, to be emotionally attached to others. It's a well-known fact that physical touch is *crucial* for us as human beings, not just for emotional health but for our very survival. Studies show that the elderly die sooner if they don't have physical touch. Babies are more likely to be diagnosed with "failure to thrive" if they're not touched.

One of the most poignant things I've witnessed as an advocate for orphans and vulnerable children is the way that a lack of physical touch affects them.

I firmly believe that orphans are meant to be adopted into permanent families, so my efforts are always focused on how to move children out of orphanages. In my work, I have visited many orphanages to learn about these precious little ones.

One particular visit stands out to me. In Kigali, Rwanda, at the Mother Teresa Home for Abandoned Babies, there were probably forty cribs lined up end to end, row after row. Some babies and toddlers reached hungrily for any available pair of arms to be held, crying in misery when they were picked up and then put back down. Their little hands clawed at ours, insisting to be picked back up. Other babies lay silently, listlessly in their cribs with their faces to the wall, already painfully aware that there were no arms *just for them.*

Without the tactile stimulation of caring parents, they don't know that they are valuable and lovable. Their intellectual development is stunted as well as their emotional development by the lack of physical affection, and many never recover from this loss.

You're probably not an orphan, but you may have been raised by parents who did not express affection easily or extravagantly. You, more than most, know how painful it is not to be connected physically or emotionally, not to be touched, hugged, embraced, not to know that somebody wants to squeeze you with the biggest bear hug they possibly can. Or maybe you were touched inappropriately and are keenly aware of the damage it caused and how it left an aching in your soul to be touched appropriately.

Don't let the cycle of disconnection or abuse continue. Don't let your parents' dysfunction or brokenness affect the succeeding generations in your family. You be the one to break the cycle! You can't erase the damage the previous generations have caused, but you can create a new pattern for yourself, your children, your grandchildren, and on down the line. Even if it's difficult for you (and it will be), work on this so that your heart and your mind and your hands can love extravagantly.

John Lubbock says, "Do not be afraid of showing your affection. Be warm and tender, thoughtful and affectionate. Men are more helped by sympathy, than by service; love is more than money, and a kind word will give more pleasure than a present."[1]

Those who love lavishly, extravagantly, find their souls flooded with joy.

Laugh and the World Laughs with You: See the Humor

You know I'm an Eeyore—serious, intense, and prone to depression. I smile and giggle with friends and family, but I don't belly laugh very easily—something has to be *really* funny to make me laugh loudly. My poor family members have bent themselves into pretzels trying to find a TV show or a movie that I think is funny; I recently learned that they flip a coin to see who has to be the sacrificial lamb and pick out the movie! Slight exaggeration, but not much.

That's one of the reasons Rick is so good for me. As a Tigger on steroids, he has brought so much laughter to my life. He makes me madder than anybody else, but he also makes me laugh like nobody else! Eeyores need people who can worm their way beneath our serious exterior and hit the funny bone. To increase our enjoyment of life, to live out that greater joy, all of us—not just Eeyores—must learn to laugh more.

Have you figured out yet that life is absurd? If it weren't absurd, *America's Funniest Home Videos* would not be on the air night after night so we can watch us make fools of ourselves!

Some people have decided that because life is absurd and there is pain in life, God must not exist. I say that *because* life is absurd and there is pain in life, I need God more than ever. If I didn't have God in my life, I couldn't survive. Yes, life is absurd. Yes, there is pain. But we run *to* God in our pain, not *away* from him.

I heard this the other day: "If something is going to be funny later, it's funny now, so go ahead and laugh about it." What a great perspective! Proverbs 15:15 says, "Every day is a terrible day for a miserable person, but a cheerful heart has a continual feast" (GW). Begin to look for the humor in your life—even if it is absurd.

Because life is absurd and there is pain in life, I need God more than ever.

A friend of mine loves to tell her most embarrassing dating moment. She met a great guy, and after they'd had a few dates, he invited her to go waterskiing with him and his brothers, whom she had never met.

After her ski run, she was trying to climb gracefully back into the boat in her cute little bikini. But as she climbed up, the bottom of her bikini got caught on a hook. As she slid into the boat, she and her bikini bottom became separated from each other. Her bikini bottom floated in the lake, while she was exposed in all her glory in front of her new boyfriend and his brothers.

If this had happened to me, I would have jumped back into the water and drowned myself! My friend? She married the guy! She says, "I figured he'd seen it all, so I might as well marry him."

When my grandmother got old, she lost muscle tone in a certain part of her anatomy, and she had a little trouble with passing gas. As she walked, she made this little toot-toot-toot sound. I would have been totally humiliated if that had happened to me, but she chose to see the humor in the situation. I remember her saying, "I am eighty years old, and if I want to toot when I walk, I will! Here I come: Toot-toot-toot!"

Going through breast cancer was not funny. The chemo I was taking guaranteed that I was going to lose all my hair. When it started to thin, I didn't want the trauma of watching it fall out in clumps, so I decided to make a preemptive strike and shave my head and start wearing a wig.

Even though I had done a lot of reading and talked to my doctor, I was just not prepared for how painful that experience would be. I can still get emotional when I'm talking about it because I have never felt more vulnerable or naked in my entire life. I did a lot of crying at first about it. But after I had worn that wig for about a year, it became less traumatic. I learned how to laugh about it.

I remember clearly one incident soon after I had finished my chemo but was still wearing my wig. I had come back to church, and I was teaching one of our women's Bible studies. It was my birthday, so all the women had loaded me down with cards and gifts. I also was holding my books and Bible, so my arms were full.

My friend Elizabeth and I were walking out to my car, and the wind was blowing pretty hard. (Can you see where this is going?) As we were walking with our arms loaded, I felt the wind catch the back of my wig. Before I knew it, my wig flew off my head and rolled end over end through the parking lot like a squirrel on the run for the border.

Elizabeth and I began to scream with laughter. Both of us ran after it, but since our arms were full, the only way I could stop this tumbling wig was to jump on it. As I picked it up, we doubled over with laughter. Where is *America's Funniest Home Videos* when you need them?

About that time I saw a big SUV come very slowly toward us. A friend of mine was driving, and her eyes were huge!

"Did you see what happened?" I asked, still laughing.

"Yes! But I didn't know whether to help you or just drive on and pretend I hadn't seen a thing."

"Well, you should have helped me chase my wig!" I told her.

A few months later I was still wearing a wig when I was asked to speak at the beginning of a women's weekend event at church. I was trying to explain to the women listening that they needed to be vulnerable. God was going to be talking to them in the upcoming days, and in order to receive what he was saying to them, they needed to let their guard down and be vulnerable before him.

I told them about the time I'd lost my wig in the church parking lot and how vulnerable I had felt. I did not plan to do this, but as I got to the place in the story when the wind took my wig off, I impulsively reached up and flipped my wig out into the audience. They shrieked. *Eeeeek!* As if I'd thrown a snake at them or something. Finally, a lady in the front row bravely picked it up and dropped it like a hot potato on the edge of the stage.

Laughter and tears come from the same deep well in the soul.

I'd already done my crying. It was time to laugh.

Laughter and tears come from the same deep well in the soul. That's why sometimes we laugh until we cry and sometimes we cry until we laugh. If you can laugh but you can't cry, you need to get some help. If you can cry but you can't laugh, you need to get some help. And if you can do neither, you definitely need to talk to a good friend or a counselor.

God intends for you to be able to weep freely and laugh uproariously, just as Jesus did. When you can recognize both the pain and the humor around you, you take another step toward knowing true joy.

The Time Is Now: Lighten Someone's Load

It's amazing how much joy can grow in your heart when you choose to be a burden bearer for someone else. Galatians 6:10 says, "As we have opportunity, let us do good to all people, especially to those who belong to the family of believers." In Hebrews 13:16, we read, "Do not forget to do good and to share with others, for with such sacrifices God is pleased."

Most of the time we go about our business with a bit of an attitude—an imaginary hand is held out in front of us acting like a protective shield that keeps others from bothering us too much, getting in our way, or interrupting our agenda for the day. We figure if we keep our heads lowered and our eyes down, we won't have to make eye contact with anyone who might mess with our plans.

Of course, we all have days that are packed to the brim, with looming deadlines and unexpected crises, that make lightening someone else's load impractical at best and downright inconvenient at worst. But this attitude can become a way of life in which we start to think that everyone exists to serve us, meet our needs, help us get our tasks done, make our lives easier—from waiters, to grocery store checkers, to bank tellers. And if they're slower than suits us, fumble something, or make a mistake, we're likely to lose our patience. "You're supposed to serve me!"

I don't know about you, but I can develop tunnel vision in a heartbeat! I can become so focused on my own stuff that I can't see what's going on in anyone else's life.

I learned this about myself in a difficult way years ago. New neighbors—newlyweds—moved into the house next to ours. The wife was bubbly and fun and warm, and I invited her over a few times just to hang out. When we sat in my kitchen and chatted and watched my kids play, I could tell there was a well of sadness inside her, but I didn't know what it was. I could see the pain in her eyes when she looked at my kids even though she seemed to really care about them.

It wasn't long before she told me that her marriage was in trouble, and they were probably going to divorce. She was heartbroken by this, and I of course was sad for her. I invited her to church, and I think she came once or twice. I told her that Rick had some tapes on marriage, and I would get them to her, but my life was busy—I was raising kids and was very active in ministry—and I had that tunnel vision thing going. I was focused on my own family and my own life. After a few weeks, I remembered my promise and got her the tapes on Rick's marriage series.

One day I was standing in my little boy's bedroom, and I could hear my neighbor sobbing in her bedroom, which was close to our house. My heart hurt for her. I thought, *I have to go talk to her this week. I just have to. Obviously, she is in a lot of pain.* But I was really busy.

Then one Saturday I was cleaning the house and doing all the Saturday chores. I was running between the house and the garage, back and forth, back and forth, all morning long. Somehow that morning, with all those trips back and forth to my garage, I didn't see that she had left an envelope on my porch. When I opened it up, I saw the marriage tapes I had given her along with a suicide note. It said, "When you read this, I will be dead. I can't go through another divorce. Please bury me in my wedding dress. Thank you for being my friend."

I did what you would have done. I freaked out. I ran to her house. I couldn't get to her front door because of the big gate in front of her house, so I banged on the garage door. I taped a message to her garage door. I left messages on her phone tearfully begging her to hold on—not to do anything to herself. I told her I cared about her and promised to help her, to be there for her—anything . . . just "please don't do anything."

I remembered that I had her husband's cell phone number, and I called him.

"Are you aware of what's going on?" I asked.

"She does this kind of stuff all the time. It's nothing," he said.

I told him, "I don't know what she's done in the past, but I think this is serious. This is real. I beg you to try to find her." But he blew me off.

About an hour later, her husband called me back, hysterical because she had shot herself in front of him and was on life support at the hospital. Although I was filled with horror at the tragedy unfolding, I asked if I could visit, and he said yes.

As I stood there holding her hand and praying for her and weeping, knowing she would be taken off life support shortly, I prayed, *God, please forgive me for being so consumed with my own family's needs that I couldn't see that this dear woman was desperately on the edge. I will not forget this. I will not. I'm not going to beat myself up about it, but I'm not going to forget it. I will use it the rest of my life to remind myself not to wait until I have more time to become a giver.*

Please understand; I'm not blaming myself for my friend's death. The motivation behind suicide is often complicated. The responsibility I take, and what I have not forgotten even after twenty-plus years, is this: If I want to become a giver, I have to become a giver now.

The people in your life today are there for a reason. You may feel you have nothing to give, that you are on empty yourself, but God will give you what you need to give to them.

In the apostle Paul's day, the church in Macedonia was in abject poverty. They were the poorest of the poor. But they heard of a need in the Jerusalem church, and they took up an offering. Paul says they gave their little offering with overflowing joy. They didn't let the fact that they had nothing stop them from being givers: "Out of the most severe trial, their overflowing joy and their extreme poverty welled up in rich generosity. For I testify that they gave as much as they were able, and even beyond their ability. Entirely on their own, they urgently pleaded with us for the privilege of sharing in this service to the saints" (2 Cor. 8:2–4).

You may be in abject poverty financially. Give a can of soup to the food pantry. You may be in abject poverty emotionally, but you can still hug somebody. You may be in abject poverty spiritually. Whisper a word of encouragement to somebody. Don't wait until you have more money, have more energy, or have it all together before you become a giver. Find the delight in serving.

Celebrating Daily

You and I have been blessed with five senses to increase our enjoyment and pleasure in what can sometimes be a very hard life. We can use our senses to make life more enjoyable for ourselves and for those closest to us by loving extravagantly, laughing at life's absurdities, and being on the alert for ways to share a friend's burden. Find a reason to celebrate *something* good daily, even on days when it would be easier just to pull the covers up over your head and shut out your problems. Henri Nouwen says, "Celebration . . . is the unceasing affirmation that underneath all the ups and downs of life there flows a solid current of joy."[2] So live, love, and laugh today in a joyous celebration of taste, touch, sight, smell, and sound.

—— PRAYER ——

Father, you have given me many gifts: the freedom to love others with touch and words, the ability to feel emotion, and people around me who are joyful. Help me to see my relationships and circumstances as you do. I want to love and laugh and live extravagantly! In the name of Jesus, who both wept and laughed, amen.

—— FOR REFLECTION AND APPLICATION ——

1. Look at the action steps on page 178 and pick one way to enjoy life through your senses.

2. Think of your daily routine with family members as they come and go from home. What can you do to add a moment of physical connection to those moments?

ELEVEN

Seeing Joy in All Things

The LORD is my strength and shield.
I trust him with all my heart.
He helps me, and my heart is filled with joy.
I burst out in songs of thanksgiving.

Psalm 28:7 NLT

For the heart that finds joy in small things, in all things, every day is a wonderful gift.

Anonymous

One trait of a joyful person is the ability to see beyond themselves and their circumstances, realizing that the eternal is more important than the temporary and making choices that reflect a hope for the future. But paradoxically, focusing on eternity also means recognizing the power of this moment. This is the time to choose to be joyful. This is the time to love. And this is the time to be grateful for the goodness God has put in the moment in front of us.

Eyes Wide Open: Practice Gratitude

When my kids were in high school, they participated in an annual mission trip to Mexico with our church. At the return of each trip, there was a reunion meeting when the students got to share with their family and friends the experiences and lessons from the trip. I waited with eager expectation each time, knowing I would hear stories of life change.

It was always the same. Student after student stood and told—many through tears—of drawing closer to God and closer to fellow students. Most of all, they talked about how thankful they were for God's material blessings to them. Many of these students had never traveled outside the US before, and they were unprepared for life the way the majority of the world experiences it on a daily basis. They stammered and stumbled as they attempted to articulate how shocked they were to witness the extent of terrible poverty, the lack of basic necessities, and the difficulty of life for the average Mexican citizen. Over and over, the words that came through their lips were, "I'm just so grateful."

I echo their sentiment. Having traveled to twenty-one countries in the past decade, I've had many opportunities to see the devastation that poverty, disease, and corrupt leadership have heaped on scores of our fellow human beings. My heart has been broken into a million pieces by the suffering. Being outside of my comfort zone has led me to say the same words the high schoolers said: "I'm just so grateful."

But you don't have to travel widely to develop a grateful heart. It starts with choosing to open your eyes to see the goodness of God today, right here, right now.

Colossians 4:2 says, "Stay alert, with your eyes wide open in gratitude" (Message). Joy is rooted in gratitude. You cannot have a joyful heart without having a grateful heart. And you cannot be a grateful person and not experience joy. Those who can praise God will experience joy. And those who are joyful will thank God. Joy and gratitude always go together.

> *Those who are joyful will thank God. Joy and gratitude always go together.*

Most of us walk around with a gigantic spiritual blindfold over our eyes, focusing on what we don't have instead of being thankful for what we do have. *Why is she married and I'm not? Why do they seem to succeed at everything they do? Why did he get a raise and I didn't? Why do they get to live there and I have to live here? Why did I pray for my loved one to be healed and he wasn't but their loved one was?* As C. S. Lewis warns, we have a tendency to "reject the good that God offers us because, at that moment, we expected some other good."[1]

Instead of being filled with gratitude for God's unbelievable goodness, kindness, and generosity to us, we are blinded by our unmet needs and accuse him of not caring for us. Joy simply cannot grow in the presence of ingratitude.

When your heart does not see the goodness of God, you're not going to say thank you to him. You're not going to experience joy because you're putting your energy into what you don't have, what you don't like about your life, what you wish was different. You ignore all that God has already done and will continue to do in your life.

In the Old Testament, we read about the Israelites building altars to say thank you to God. They built not just the altar in the tabernacle and the temple but also stone monuments in the midst of their travels to thank God for a way he had shown up in their lives.

In Joshua 4, for example, God told Joshua to choose twelve men, one from each tribe of Israel, to take twelve stones from the middle of the Jordan River and place them where the priests who had carried the ark of the covenant had stood.

After this was done, Joshua said to the Israelites:

In the future when your descendants ask their fathers, "What do these stones mean?" tell them, "Israel crossed the Jordan on dry ground." For the Lord your God dried up the Jordan before you until you had crossed over. The Lord your God did to the Jordan what he had done to the Red Sea when he dried it up before us until we had crossed over. He did this so that all the peoples of the earth might know that the hand of the Lord is powerful and so that you might always fear the Lord your God. (Josh. 4:21–24)

For generations to come, people passed that pile of stones, an altar that represented something God had done. God knew they were a forgetful people. But they obeyed God's command to mark his presence in their lives so that they, and those who followed them, would remember his goodness.

You and I are not likely to build a stone monument in our backyard this week. I challenge you, though, to take a walk in the coming days and find a rock—something big enough that it captures your attention when you see it. Bring it home, put it on your desk or kitchen counter, and let it be a visible reminder to say thank you to God for being present in your life. That stone of remembrance will bring you back to a place of being a grateful person. Then you can praise God as King David did in Psalm 126:3: "The LORD has done great things for us, and we are filled with joy."

Some of you might be ready to go even deeper into practicing gratitude—if for no other reason than to increase your own level of joy. For years my sister-in-love, Chaundel, has kept a gratitude journal, writing down one item every day to thank God for. Some days the "thanks" is as small as, "Thanks, God, for Taco Tuesday," or, "Thank you, God, for rain," or, "Thank you, God, for my patient husband." It's no wonder she has both a grateful and a joyful heart.

You Are Here: Live in the Moment

One of my dearest friends, Dee, has five children, two of them with cerebral palsy and one of them, Meagan, with severe cerebral palsy.

One day, when Meagan was younger, Dee was down on the floor with her other four children. They were laughing and tickling, doing all the silly things that kids love to do. Meagan was just sitting in her wheelchair, wistfully watching the shenanigans.

Dee decided to lift Meagan out of her wheelchair and plop her right down on the floor in the middle of her siblings. Meagan's muscles are very stiff, and she has almost no ability to control her own movements, so sitting on the floor with her roughhousing siblings left her in a relatively vulnerable position. But the minute Dee put her on the floor, her face lit up with a smile the size of Montana. Her delight in being in the heap of goofy siblings was palpable. Dee stood on the edge of the tumbling heap of precious children and said to herself, "I am *loving* this moment!"

Did Dee have to put Meagan back in the wheelchair a few minutes later? Yes. Did being on the ground with her siblings heal Meagan's physical condition? No. Did that moment of playfulness take away the sting of limitations or pain or hardship? No. But when Dee opened up her heart to live in the moment, she opened up her heart to joy.

A few months later, I was walking on the beach with one of my children who was facing some serious challenges. He wasn't in school like his siblings—he had to do things differently. I was grieving for what was going on in his life and mine.

We had gone to see the tide pools on a day after a huge storm, so driftwood and trash littered the sand. The beach wasn't pretty. There were dark clouds in the sky that matched my mood. I kept thinking, *I don't like this, God. I want him to be enjoying normal life like other kids his age. This is so sad.*

I had a sudden memory of the conversation Dee and I had had months earlier. I pushed the pause button on my pensive thoughts and looked at my son. In that moment, he was laughing as he skipped down the beach, dodging the waves and chasing a seagull. I said, *God, I am loving this moment!* The situation didn't change; the challenges remained as daunting as they had been minutes before, but by consciously reframing the pain, I was at peace. Loving a moment doesn't remove the pain, but it does make room for joy.

To experience joy on a daily basis, learn what it means to live in the moment. Notice I said *in*, not *for*. To live *for* the moment is irresponsible and leads to decisions you may regret. You may already have a testimony of what it meant for you to live *for* the moment.

Living *in* the moment helps us recognize that God can be found in this moment, whether it contains joy or sorrow. As a perfectionist, I'm always waiting for a *perfect* moment before I enjoy it. But nothing is ever perfect! That's why the Bible encourages us to "make the most of every opportunity" for doing good (Eph. 5:16 NLT). Make the most of this moment. Make the most of this opportunity to do good. Make the most of this opportunity to choose joy.

The problem is, we're greedy. We don't want just *moments*. We want weeks and days and months and years. We want a lifetime. And if we can't have huge blocks of time that are wonderful and stress-free, we decide we can't be joyful.

Yet sometimes moments are all we have. You and I can decide that we have *this* moment, and we will choose to love it. We're not denying that we have problems. We're not saying our lives are wrapped neatly with a bow on top and we have everything figured out. It just means that this moment is a gift from God, and we will cherish it. We will love it.

Mike Mason says, "A decision to rejoice in the present changes not only the present, it also changes my view of the past and ignites my future with hope."[2]

I've stopped demanding that a moment last longer than it can. I don't require a moment to be anything other than what it is: a brief span of time that has been given by a gracious Father. I will wring every bit of pleasure out of *this* moment because I don't know when the next one will come.

We're rarely satisfied with today; we spend too much time regretting the unrepeatable past and wishing we could get a do-over, or we waste our energy on worry and anxiety about the unknowable future. Either way, TODAY is ignored or minimized.

In Psalm 118:24, we read, "This is the day the LORD has made. We will rejoice and be glad in it." Try this exercise: Repeat this verse out loud, emphasizing a different word each time.

> This is the day the LORD has made. I will rejoice and be glad in it.
> This *is* the day the LORD has made. I will rejoice and be glad in it.
> This is the *day* the LORD has made. I will rejoice and be glad in it.
> This is the day the *LORD* has made. I will rejoice and be glad in it.
> This is the day the LORD has *made*. I will rejoice and be glad in it.

You'll be amazed at how this verse comes alive. Something will begin to shift deep in your soul, and you will stop insisting that God give you days, weeks, months, years, a lifetime. You'll stop looking for the perfect time to start living. You will begin to enjoy the moments of your life, starting now.

If you want to increase the level of joy in your heart, you've got to decide that whether you are in pain or not, this is the moment you are in. God can be found in this moment.

The Choice to Rejoice: Find the Bless in the Mess

Corrie ten Boom was a Dutch woman who, with her family, hid Jewish neighbors from the Nazis during World War II.

When a Dutch informant gave them away, the Ten Boom family was arrested and sent to concentration camps.

In her book *The Hiding Place*, Corrie tells of her experience with her sister, Betsie, at a notorious concentration camp in Germany called Ravensbruck. (Betsie later died there, just a few days before Corrie was released.)

When Corrie and Betsie arrived at the barracks at Ravensbruck, Betsie thanked God for every aspect of the miserable place, including the fleas that were rampant in the thin, dirty blankets. Corrie could thank God for having a Bible, for being with her sister, and even for the women around them, but she had trouble thanking God for fleas.

Corrie and Betsie wanted to lead a Bible study for the women in their overcrowded, suffocating barracks. If there is a hellhole on earth, it is a concentration camp. And if there were ever women in need of knowing there was a God who loved them and had not forgotten their name, it was those women. But Corrie knew that if the guards found them leading a study, Corrie and her sister might be starved, tortured, or even killed.

So when they began holding the studies, they were cautious. Soon they found, however, that no guards disturbed them. Even though guards seemed to be present for every moment of the day, they never seemed to bother with that part of the barracks.

Betsie discovered why: The guards didn't want to get close to those horrible fleas. Women were allowed to study the Bible, pray, and praise God because of those fleas. The sisters discovered that there *was* a reason to thank God for everything.

I'm not sure I could thank God for being covered with fleas. But Betsie lived out our definition of joy: She had the settled assurance that God was in control of all the details of her life, the quiet confidence that ultimately everything would be all right, and the determined choice to praise God in all things. She made the *choice* to rejoice.

A few years ago, I heard a professional stress consultant say that one of the ways to decrease stress and increase joy is to find the "bless in the mess." Finding the bless in the mess is a secular way of saying Romans 8:28: "We know that in all things God works for the good of those who love him." Even in our worst messes, we can find blessings if we look for them.

Who finds the blessings in the mess? The naturally cheerful, happy people? Maybe. The people who are successful, attractive, and talented? Not necessarily.

The people who find the blessings in the mess are those who intentionally seek them. In every masterpiece, there is a flaw; in everything good on earth, there is something not quite right. But the parallel train tracks of good and bad also mean that in everything bad we can find something praiseworthy. As it says in Philippians 4:8, "Summing it all up, friends, I'd say you'll do best by filling your minds and meditating on things true, noble, reputable, authentic, compelling, gracious—the best, not the worst; the beautiful, not the ugly; things to praise, not things to curse" (Message).

Filling our minds with good things does not mean living in denial. It means looking at the messes of our lives and finding the places where joy is hiding. Those two train tracks of joy and sorrow run inseparably until that day when we will meet Jesus Christ. As you and I live in the meantime, we look for the blessings, we look for what is right.

A widow who recently lost her husband told me of an unexpected joy in her life. "You're not going to believe this," she said, "but one of my treasures right now is my bedroom. My husband had remodeled our room shortly before he died. Now when I walk in, I see what he created for me. I see his love for me spread out over everything he did. And when I walk into our bedroom, I say out loud, 'Thank you. Thank you for showing your love to me.'"

The people who find the blessings in the mess are those who intentionally seek them.

Most of us would assume that walking into that bedroom would bring a new wave of grief for all she is missing. But this is a woman who has decided in her mature walk with God that she is going to look for joy, a treasure even in her messiest darkness.

Often when bad things happen to us, the first words out of our mouths are, "Why?" or, "Why me?" Philip Bernstein said, "We have no right to ask when a sorrow comes, 'Why did this happen to me?' unless we ask the same question for every joy that comes our way."[3]

I don't know if you've noticed it or not, but God rarely answers that question—at least not in words we want to hear. As C. S. Lewis says in his novel *Till We Have Faces*, "I know now, Lord, why you utter no answer. You are yourself the answer. Before your face questions die away."[4]

Some of the messes you and I are in we brought on ourselves. Some of them were caused by other people. Some of them just happened because we live in a broken world. But here's one truth I'm certain of: It is out of the messes of our lives that ministry comes. It is out of the messes we think can never be redeemed, can never contain a hidden blessing, that God wants to bring ministry. And from that ministry and that intimacy with God come great joy.

My own life has had a lot of messes that held a lot of blessings. My marriage started out very, very hard. Some years Rick and I didn't know if we would make it. We were committed to each other, believing that the promises we made to each other before God were binding, but we couldn't seem to overcome our differences. We have had to forgive each other for so much, to come back time after time and say, "Let's start again."

The blessing in that mess is that when women come to me and say, "You can't possibly know what it's like to live in a marriage where you're not sure it's going to work. You can't tell me I should stay in my marriage or I should work on it, because you don't know," I can look at them and say, "Yes, I do. I know some of what you're going through. And I know that if God can take very different people like Rick and me and build a beautiful, stable, happy relationship, he can do that for you as well." There was a blessing hidden in that mess.

When the son of our church janitor molested me when I was a little girl, it seemed like nothing more than a mess. It created years of problems and brokenness. But I finally sought counseling, and over time, God has repaired much of the damage. Now there is rarely a time when I speak to a group of women when a woman doesn't come up to me at the end of my talk and say, "I've never told anybody this before, but I went through a similar experience. If God can heal you, maybe he can heal me." And that mess I went through gives hope to others.

Having breast cancer and melanoma was definitely a mess, but as I have already mentioned, being sick was ultimately a blessing, opening doors of ministry that might otherwise have remained closed.

This much I can tell you: I have discovered a more vibrant, richer walk with Jesus Christ than I have had at any other point in my life. My soul resonates with the apostle Paul in 2 Corinthians 7:11: "And now, isn't it wonderful all the ways in which this distress has goaded you closer to God? You're more alive, more concerned, more sensitive, more reverent, more human, more passionate, more responsible. Looked at from any angle, you've come out of this with purity of heart" (Message).

Right now I'm searching for the blessing in the mess of mental illness as I pray for healing for a loved one. Trusting God has not yet resulted in healing, and once again, I find myself up against the Red Sea—hemmed in from behind by a cruel enemy I can't control. Unanswered prayer and unclear "blesses in the mess" are teaching me about radical, audacious trust in a God who remains largely a mystery to me. But here's the bottom line for me: I would rather walk every day in the darkness with a God who remains a mystery than in the light with a God I completely understand. Why? Because it's only in the messes that we start to develop the vibrant faith in God that leads to daily joy.

Passing the Joy On

A new friend, Becky Johnson, articulately sums up the power of the potential each of us has to bring joy into the lives of others as we cooperate with God's process of transforming us from people of sorrow into people of joy.

"I recently came across a photo my husband, Greg, took of Crater Lake, which is the purest, bluest blue, deepest lake in the US. I recall the otherworldly quiet around it. When

I visualize the word *peace*, this is the picture that comes to mind now.

"This lake was formed by a volcanic eruption that left a huge hole open to receive rain and snow until this gorgeous place of tranquility was formed.

"Isn't this a fabulous metaphor for life? It seems that crisis, failure, eruption (a 'blowing up of what was before') happens at some point to most of us, hopefully leaving us broken open, with room to be filled, slowly but surely, with fresh new rain from heaven. You are changed, and if you let God have his way, you eventually become a place of depth, beauty, and serenity for others."

Isn't that what we want? Don't we all aspire to be people who leave marks of blessing on the lives of those we touch? Don't we all desire to see the broken places in us healed and restored so that we can be a part of healing and restoring others? Don't we yearn to be an inspiration to others who are watching our lives? Don't we wish from the core of who we are to be on somebody's short list of those who live out God's call to choose joy—no matter what? I think we do.

Wishing and yearning and desiring and aspiring won't make it happen. But if we choose to become that kind of a person, we can.

By the grace of the Lord Jesus Christ, and the love of God, and the fellowship of the Holy Spirit, we can become women of joy.

—— **PRAYER** ——

Father, I'm afraid. Afraid to believe that I could be different, that I could change. Afraid to believe that you could replace my mourning with dancing and that I could become someone who feels the sadness of life but still chooses to pursue joy. I want to live today, right now, as someone who chooses joy. Give me strength and courage to look for your blessings on this journey. In Jesus's name, amen.

FOR REFLECTION AND APPLICATION

1. Where have you forgotten to be grateful to God? Consider beginning a gratitude journal and writing down one blessing every day for thirty days. It can be as simple as a word or a phrase.

2. Take a minute to think about the day before you. Think about times in your day when you can slow down and fully live in the moments God gives you with family, friends, and him. Commit to embracing each moment in its imperfection.

Conclusion

May the God of hope fill you with all joy and peace as you trust in him, so that you may overflow with hope by the power of the Holy Spirit.

Romans 15:13

As you've read this book, maybe you've been unpleasantly surprised that you're not as strong or as kind or as joyful as you thought you were. I know what you mean—I'm not either. But rather than give up on the search for joy, let's allow that reality to bring us to a place of hope—hope that God is already at work within us, that those stirrings in our souls actually mean joy can be ours.

My friends, if we are going to experience joy in this lifetime, there's only one possible way: We will have to choose it. We will have to choose it *in spite of* unbelievable circumstances. We will have to choose it *in the middle of* a situation that seems too hard to bear. We will have to choose it *even if* our worst nightmare comes true.

This isn't what we want to hear. We keep trying to line up all the little ducks in a row, to smooth out the rough spots, and to shore up all the wobbly places, still convinced that if we get our act together, we finish the huge project, our health clears up, we get a raise, or we can just get things *right,* we can finally be joyful.

But the ducks won't cooperate; they won't stay in the row. The rough spots just get rougher, and the wobbly places sometimes threaten to completely topple our carefully constructed lives. I'm pretty sure this is true for all of us, not just for the perfectionists. No, if you're going to experience joy, you must choose it—in spite of, even if, and in the middle of everything else.

So ask yourself, What unchangeable circumstance stands in the way of me choosing joy? What is happening now that may or may not change? What fears for the future keep me from choosing joy? Where am I missing the boat?

Whatever you do, don't miss joy. Don't miss the reason for your existence. Spend a few minutes now in quietness and talk to God from your heart. Say something like this:

> *God, thank you for your love and passion for me and for accepting me into your family through Jesus Christ. I'm so amazed to be your beloved, but I'm eternally grateful.*
>
> *Thank you for Jesus Christ. His life as both a man of sorrows and a man of joy gives me permission to seek a life of joy for myself. Thank you for your Holy Spirit, who graciously gave me the gift of joy as part of my spiritual inheritance, my birthright; I choose to fight for my right to experience joy.*
>
> *I choose to stop digging my own broken cisterns that can't hold water. I choose to no longer look at people,*

places, positions, possessions, and my personality to find joy.

I choose instead to find my joy in the only true source of joy: YOU! You are the only one who has soul-quenching springs of living water that will never leave me dry.

I choose to seek the eternal over the temporary every time. I choose to meditate on who you are so that I can align my value system with yours, God, with the value system of heaven. That is where I will choose to place my mind and my thoughts.

I choose to nurture joy in myself and in the lives of those you have placed in my path. I choose to be a joy builder instead of a joy killer. I choose to grow in the heart attitudes of grace, trust, balance, acceptance, positive thoughts of others, nonjudgmental love, empathy, and appreciation.

I choose to make changes in my daily life that help me live a life of joy. I choose to value myself the way you value me, to intentionally seek out joy mentors, to not get caught up in the small irritations of daily life. I choose to love extravagantly, to take advantage of the pleasures my senses provide, to laugh from my belly, and to become a giver today, not someday off in the future.

I choose to live with a grateful heart, eyes wide open to see your goodness. I choose to love every moment of life you give to me, whether that moment contains sorrow or joy. I choose to look for you and for joy in every messy circumstance that you allow.

I choose to develop a settled assurance that you are in control of all the details of my life. I choose to be *quietly confident that ultimately everything will be all right. And I choose to praise you in all things, even the things I cannot understand. I trust you, God.*

I courageously choose joy, because happiness will never be enough.

I choose joy!

Acknowledgments

To my amazing family: Rick, I'll always be grateful for the way you cheer me on, eager to see me use my gifts in God's kingdom. Because you know the process of writing a book, you're patient when I'm distracted and absorbed in words and ideas. Coming home every day to your love for me is one of life's best gifts. You are a solid rock of stability when so much around us changes. To Amy, Tommy, Josh, Jaime, and Matthew, thank you for believing in me and for urging me to "just do it, Mom." With each passing year, I grow to love you more and more! I am *so* proud of the people you are becoming—full of integrity, compassion, and hope. Oh, by the way, thanks for the grandkids! Momma, can I please be like you when I grow up? I hope I'm as passionately in love with Jesus and his children as you are when I'm eighty-eight. What a role model you are! Andy, Zac, Tom, Chaundel, Ryan, Brittany, Alyssa, and Luke—no one has ever had sweeter siblings, nieces, and nephews than I have!

To my incredible office staff: Paulette, Joy, and Jeanne, you make my life possible! You've prayed for me, laughed with me, made sure my iced-tea glass was full, handled my schedule, run errands, encouraged me when I hit the wall, babysat my grandkids, and, most of all, you have loved me. Where would I be without you?

To my prayer team: You know who you are; you're the ones who have carried me to God when I could barely drag myself out of bed. You've been there in the darkness and in the radiant sunshine, faithfully interceding at all hours of the day and night. There have been a few days when knowing you were talking to God on behalf of me and my family made the difference between giving up and holding on.

To the women of Saddleback Church: We've been walking together on the parallel train tracks of joy and sorrow for more than thirty years. It has been the highest honor to spend my life with you.

To the capable and caring staff of Baker Books and Revell: Jack Kuhatschek, Jennifer Leep, Twila Bennett, Michele Misiak, Janelle Mahlmann, Deonne Lindsey, Claudia Marsh, and Dave Lewis and his excellent sales team. I appreciate your willingness to turn a dream into a reality. Andrea Doering, you're a superb editor; so glad you were mine!

Notes

Chapter 1 Seeking a Life of Joy

1. Shannon Royce, Chosen Families.org, http://chosenfamilies.org/welcome
-to-chosen-families/.

2. John Eldredge, *Waking the Dead* (Nashville: Thomas Nelson, 2003), 34.

3. Lewis Smedes, *How Can It Be All Right When Everything Is All Wrong?*, rev. ed. (Wheaton: Harold Shaw, 1999), 27, 43.

4. Sailhamer's exact quote is, "Joy is that deep settled confidence that God is in control of every area of my life." Cited in Tim Hansel, *You Gotta Keep Dancin'* (Colorado Springs: David C Cook, 1998), 54.

Chapter 2 Showing Our True Colors

1. Ronald Dunn, *When Heaven Is Silent: Trusting God When Life Hurts* (Fort Washington, PA: CLC Publications, 2008), 27.

Chapter 3 Rediscovering Jesus, the Man of Joy

1. Matthew 11:16–19 Message.

Chapter 4 Drinking from Dry Wells

1. Larry Crabb, *Inside Out* (Colorado Springs: NavPress, 1988), 54.

2. M. Craig Barnes, *When God Interrupts: Finding New Life through Un-wanted Change* (Downers Grove, IL: InterVarsity, 1996), 124.

Chapter 5 Adopting Heaven's Value System

1. Padre Pio, http://stdavidsanglican.com/prayermeditation.htm.

2. Carol Kent, *When I Lay My Isaac Down* (Colorado Springs: NavPress, 2004), 29.

Chapter 6 Believing Even in Darkness

1. Henri Nouwen, *Can You Drink the Cup?* (Notre Dame, IN: Ave Maria Press, 2006), 51.

Part 3 Joy Is a Condition of My Heart

1. Mike Mason, *Champagne for the Soul* (Vancouver, BC: Regent College Publishing, 2006), 26.

Chapter 7 Nurturing Joy in Yourself

1. C. S. Lewis, *The World's Last Night: And Other Essays* (New York: Harcourt, 1960), 86.

2. Sarah Young, *Jesus Calling* (Nashville: Thomas Nelson, 2004), 59.

3. Annie Dillard, *The Writing Life* (New York: Harper & Row, 1989), 32.

4. J. R. R. Tolkien, *The Fellowship of the Ring* (Boston: Houghton Mifflin, 1966), 50.

5. Richard Carlson, *Don't Sweat the Small Stuff—And It's All Small Stuff* (New York: Hyperion, 1996), 9.

Chapter 8 Nurturing Joy in Others

1. C. S. Lewis, *The Screwtape Letters*, rev. ed. (New York: Macmillan, 1982), 17.

2. Taylor Caldwell, *The Listener* (New York: Doubleday, 1960), 9.

Part 4 Joy Is a Choice of My Behavior

1. Katia Hetter, "This Is the World's Happiest Country in 2019," CNN Travel, March 26, 2019, https://www.cnn.com/travel/article/worlds-happiest-countries -united-nations-2019/index.html.

2. Hetter, "World's Happiest Country in 2019."

3. Hetter, "World's Happiest Country in 2019."

Chapter 9 Getting Back to Basics

1. For more information on studies and research, visit the Centers for Disease Control and Prevention website at www.cdc.gov/physicalactivity/everyone/health /index.html.

2. Paul Tournier, cited in Tim Hansel, *You Gotta Keep Dancin'*, 104.

Chapter 10 Loving and Laughing Together

1. Sir John Lubbock, *The Use of Life* (Charleston, SC: BiblioBazaar, 2009), 197.